WASHINGTON DC
RESTAURANT GUIDE

RESTAURANTS, BARS AND CAFES
Your Guide to Authentic Regional Eats

GUIDE BOOK FOR TOURIST

WASHINGTON DC RESTAURANT GUIDE 2022
Best Rated Restaurants in Washington DC

© Herbert I. Gilmore
© E.G.P. Editorial

Printed in USA.

ISBN-13: 9798503783438

WASHINGTON DC RESTAURANT GUIDE
The Most Recommended Restaurants in the City

*This directory is dedicated to the Business Owners and Managers
who provide the experience that the locals and tourists enjoy.
Thanks you very much for all that you do and thank for being the "People Choice".*

*Thanks to everyone that posts their reviews online and
the amazing reviews sites that make our life easier.*

*The places listed in this book are the most positively reviewed
and recommended by locals and travelers from around the world.*

*Thank you for your time and enjoy the directory that is
designed with locals and tourist in mind!*

TOP 500
RESTAURANTS

Ranked from #1 to #500

#1
The Pig
Cuisines: American, Cocktail Bars
Average price: Modest
Area: Logan Circle, Downtown
Address: 1320 14th St NW
Washington, DC 20005
Phone: (202) 290-2821

#2
Founding Farmers - D.C
Cuisines: American, Coffee & Tea,
Breakfast & Brunch
Average price: Modest
Area: Foggy Bottom, Downtown
Address: 1924 Pennsylvania Ave NW
Washington, DC 20006
Phone: (202) 822-8783

#3
Reren
Cuisines: Ramen, Asian Fusion, Chinese
Average price: Modest
Area: Chinatown
Address: 817 7th St NW
Washington, DC 20001
Phone: (202) 290-3677

#4
Cherry Blossom Pub
Cuisines: Pubs, Pop-Up Restaurants
Average price: Modest
Area: Shaw
Address: 1843 7th St NW
Washington, DC 20001
Phone: (202) 316-9396

#5
Spark
Cuisines: Barbeque,
Caribbean, Venues & Event Spaces
Average price: Modest
Area: Bloomingdale
Address: 1626 N Capitol St NW
Washington, DC 20002
Phone: (202) 299-9128

#6
Farmbird
Cuisines: Chicken Shop, American
Average price: Modest
Area: H Street Corridor/Atlas Distric
Address: 625A H St NE
Washington, DC 20002
Phone: (202) 506-6778

#7
Rose's Luxury
Cuisines: American, Italian
Average price: Expensive
Area: Capitol Hill
Address: 717 8th St SE
Washington, DC 20003
Phone: (202) 580-8889

#8
The Fainting Goat
Cuisines: American, Bars
Average price: Modest
Area: U Street Corridor
Address: 1330 U St NW
Washington, DC 20009
Phone: (202) 735-0344

#9
Bandit Taco
Cuisines: Mexican
Average price: Modest
Area: U Street Corridor
Address: 1946 New Hampshire Ave NW
Washington, DC 20009
Phone: (202) 609-8127

#10
Tiger Fork
Cuisines: Chinese, Hong Kong
Average price: Modest
Area: Shaw, Downtown
Address: 922 N St NW
Washington, DC 20001
Phone: (202) 733-1152

#11
Il Canale
Cuisines: Italian, Pizza
Average price: Modest
Area: Georgetown
Address: 1065 31st St NW
Washington, DC 20007
Phone: (202) 337-4444

#12
B DC Penn Quarter
Cuisines: Burgers, Bars, American
Average price: Modest
Area: Penn Quarter
Address: 801 Pennsylvania Ave NW
Washington, DC 20004
Phone: (202) 808-8720

#13
Churchkey
Cuisines: American, Lounges
Average price: Modest
Area: Logan Circle, Downtown
Address: 1337 14th St NW
Washington, DC 20005
Phone: (202) 567-2576

#14
Chloe
Cuisines: American, Modern European
Average price: Expensive
Area: Navy Yard
Address: 1331 4th St SE
Washington, DC 20003
Phone: (202) 313-7007

#15
Sakuramen
Cuisines: Asian Fusion, Ramen, Korean
Average price: Modest
Area: Adams Morgan
Address: 2441 18th St NW
Washington, DC 20009
Phone: (202) 656-5285

#16
Pennsylvania 6 DC
Cuisines: American, Seafood, Cocktail Bars
Average price: Expensive
Area: Downtown
Address: 1350 Eye St NW
Washington, DC 20005
Phone: (202) 796-1600

#17
Honeysuckle
Cuisines: American
Average price: Expensive
Area: Downtown
Address: 1990 M St NW
Washington, DC 20036
Phone: (202) 659-1990

#18
Duke's Counter
Cuisines: Burgers, Pubs, Sandwiches
Average price: Modest
Area: Woodley Park
Address: 3000 Connecticut Ave NW
Washington, DC 20008
Phone: (202) 733-4808

#19
Tail Up Goat
Cuisines: Cocktail Bars, American, Italian
Average price: Expensive
Area: Adams Morgan
Address: 1827 Adams Mill Rd NW
Washington, DC 20009
Phone: (202) 986-9600

#20
Ivy City Smokehouse Tavern
Cuisines: Seafood, Smokehouse, Bars
Average price: Modest
Area: Ivy City
Address: 1356 Okie St NE
Washington, DC 20002
Phone: (202) 529-3300

#21
Clyde's Of Georgetown
Cuisines: American, Bars
Average price: Modest
Area: Georgetown
Address: 3236 M St NW
Washington, DC 20007
Phone: (202) 333-9180

#22
Convivial
Cuisines: American, French, Bars
Average price: Modest
Area: Shaw
Address: 801 O St NW
Washington, DC 20001
Phone: (202) 525-2870

#23
Momofuku CCDC
Cuisines: American, Bars
Average price: Modest
Area: Downtown
Address: 1090 I St NW
Washington, DC 20001
Phone: (202) 602-1832

#24
Blue Duck Tavern
Cuisines: American,
Breakfast & Brunch, Cocktail Bars
Average price: Expensive
Area: West End
Address: 1201 24th St NW
Washington, DC 20037
Phone: (202) 419-6755

#25
Toki Underground
Cuisines: Ramen
Average price: Modest
Area: H Street Corridor/Atlas District
Address: 1234 H St NE
Washington, DC 20002
Phone: (202) 388-3086

#26
Seoulspice
Cuisines: Korean, Gluten-Free, Comfort Food
Average price: Inexpensive
Area: Noma
Address: 145 N St NE
Washington, DC 20002
Phone: (202) 792-8879

#27
Da Hong Pao
Cuisines: Cantonese, Dim Sum
Average price: Modest
Area: Logan Circle, Downtown
Address: 1409 14th St NW
Washington, DC 20005
Phone: (202) 846-7229

#28
Chiko
Cuisines: Chinese, Korean
Average price: Modest
Area: Capitol Hill
Address: 423 8th St SE
Washington, DC 20003
Phone: (202) 558-9934

#29
Chaplin's
Cuisines: Cocktail Bars, Ramen
Average price: Modest
Area: Shaw, Downtown
Address: 1501 9th St NW
Washington, DC 20001
Phone: (202) 644-8806

#30
Stoney's On L
Cuisines: American, Lounges
Average price: Modest
Area: Downtown
Address: 2101 L St NW
Washington, DC 20037
Phone: (202) 721-0019

#31
Grand Trunk
Cuisines: Asian Fusion, Pakistani, Indian
Average price: Modest
Area: Penn Quarter
Address: 641 Indiana Ave NW
Washington, DC 20004
Phone: (202) 347-3293

#33
The Dabney
Cuisines: American, Desserts, Cocktail Bars
Average price: Expensive
Area: Shaw, Downtown
Address: 122 Blagden Aly NW
Washington, DC 20001
Phone: (202) 450-1015

#32
Al Volo
Cuisines: Italian
Average price: Modest
Area: Adams Morgan
Address: 1790 Columbia Rd NW
Washington, DC 20009
Phone: (202) 758-0759

#34
Filomena Ristorante
Cuisines: Italian, Wine Bars
Average price: Expensive
Area: Georgetown
Address: 1063 Wisconsin Ave NW
Washington, DC 20007
Phone: (202) 338-8800

#35
Radiator
Cuisines: Tapas/Small Plates,
Gastropubs, Cocktail Bars
Average price: Modest
Area: Logan Circle, Downtown
Address: 1430 Rhode Island Ave NW
Washington, DC 20005
Phone: (202) 742-3150

#36
Hot N Juicy Crawfish
Cuisines: Seafood, Cajun/Creole
Average price: Modest
Area: Woodley Park
Address: 2651 Connecticut Ave NW
Washington, DC 20008
Phone: (202) 299-9448

#37
JINYA Ramen Bar
Cuisines: Ramen, Izakaya
Average price: Modest
Area: Logan Circle, Downtown
Address: 1336 14th St NW
Washington, DC 20005
Phone: (202) 588-8560

#38
Barrel
Cuisines: American,
Cocktail Bars, Breakfast & Brunch
Average price: Modest
Area: Capitol Hill
Address: 613 Pennsylvania Ave SE
Washington, DC 20003
Phone: (202) 543-3622

#39
Quill
Cuisines: Bars, American
Average price: Expensive
Area: Downtown
Address: 1200 16th St NW
Washington, DC 20036
Phone: (202) 448-2300

#40
Floriana
Cuisines: Italian
Average price: Modest
Area: Dupont Circle
Address: 1602 17th St NW
Washington, DC 20009
Phone: (202) 667-5937

#41
Ambar
Cuisines: Modern European
Average price: Modest
Area: Capitol Hill
Address: 523 8th St SE
Washington, DC 20003
Phone: (202) 813-3039

#42
Purple Patch
Cuisines: Filipino, American, Cocktail Bars
Average price: Modest
Area: Mount Pleasant
Address: 3155 Mt Pleasant St NW
Washington, DC 20010
Phone: (202) 299-0022

#43
Masala Story
Cuisines: Indian
Average price: Modest
Area: Brookland
Address: 3301 12th St NE
Washington, DC 20017
Phone: (202) 885-9810

#44
Baan Thai
Cuisines: Sushi Bars, Thai, Cocktail Bars
Average price: Modest
Area: Logan Circle, Downtown
Address: 1326 14th St NW
Washington, DC 20005
Phone: (202) 588-5889

#45
Oki Bowl DC
Cuisines: Ramen, Asian Fusion
Average price: Modest
Area: Downtown
Address: 1817 M St NW
Washington, DC 20036
Phone: (202) 750-6703

#46
Hen Quarter
Cuisines: Southern, Breakfast & Brunch
Average price: Modest
Area: Penn Quarter
Address: 750 E St NW
Washington, DC 20004
Phone: (202) 248-7036

#47
Primrose
Cuisines: French, Bars, Comfort Food
Average price: Modest
Area: Brookland
Address: 3000 12th St NE
Washington, DC 20017
Phone: (202) 248-4558

#48
The Pub & The People
Cuisines: American, Pubs
Average price: Modest
Area: Bloomingdale
Address: 1648 N Capitol St NW
Washington, DC 20002
Phone: (202) 234-1800

#49
Diet Starts Monday
Cuisines: American, Bars
Average price: Modest
Area: U Street Corridor
Address: 2005 14th St NW
Washington, DC 20009
Phone: (240) 232-6338

#50
Whaley's
Cuisines: Bars, Seafood,
Venues & Event Spaces
Average price: Modest
Area: Navy Yard
Address: 301 Water St SE
Washington, DC 20003
Phone: (202) 484-8800

#51
Thip Khao
Cuisines: Laotian
Average price: Modest
Area: Columbia Heights
Address: 3462 14th St NW
Washington, DC 20010
Phone: (202) 387-5426

#52
Right Proper Brewing Company
Cuisines: Gastropubs, Breweries
Average price: Modest
Area: Shaw
Address: 624 T St NW
Washington, DC 20001
Phone: (202) 607-2337

#53
Kyirisan
Cuisines: French, Chinese, Bars
Average price: Expensive
Area: Shaw
Address: 1924 8th St NW
Washington, DC 20001
Phone: (202) 525-2942

#54
Bonchon Navy Yard
Cuisines: Chicken Wings,
Korean, Asian Fusion
Average price: Modest
Area: Navy Yard
Address: 1015 Half St SE
Washington, DC 20003
Phone: (202) 488-4000

#55
Copycat Co
Cuisines: Cocktail Bars, Chinese
Average price: Modest
Area: H Street Corridor/Atlas District
Address: 1110 H St NE
Washington, DC 20002
Phone: (202) 241-1952

#56
Luke's Lobster Penn Quarter
Cuisines: Seafood
Average price: Modest
Area: Penn Quarter
Address: 624 E St NW
Washington, DC 20004
Phone: (202) 347-3355

#57
Le Diplomate
Cuisines: Brasseries, French, Cafes
Average price: Expensive
Area: Logan Circle
Address: 1601 14th St NW
Washington, DC 20009
Phone: (202) 332-3333

#58
Donburi
Cuisines: Japanese
Average price: Modest
Area: Downtown
Address: 1134 19th St NW
Washington, DC 20036
Phone: (202) 296-7941

#59
Ghibellina
Cuisines: Italian, Cocktail Bars, Pizza
Average price: Modest
Area: Logan Circle
Address: 1610 14th St NW
Washington, DC 20009
Phone: (202) 803-2389

#60
La Puerta Verde
Cuisines: Mexican
Average price: Modest
Area: Ivy City
Address: 2001 Fenwick St NE
Washington, DC 20002
Phone: (202) 290-1875

#61
Dumplings & Beyond
Cuisines: Chinese
Average price: Modest
Area: Glover Park
Address: 2400 Wisconsin Ave NW
Washington, DC 20007
Phone: (202) 338-3815

#62
Rice Bar
Cuisines: Korean, Delis
Average price: Modest
Area: Downtown
Address: 1015 15th St NW
Washington, DC 20005
Phone: (202) 589-0030

#63
Due South
Cuisines: Southern, Barbeque
Average price: Modest
Area: Navy Yard
Address: 301 Water St SE
Washington, DC 20003
Phone: (202) 479-4616

#64
Open City
Cuisines: American, Diners, Pizza
Average price: Modest
Area: Woodley Park
Address: 2331 Calvert St NW
Washington, DC 20008
Phone: (202) 332-2331

#65
Brookland's Finest
Cuisines: American, Bars
Average price: Modest
Area: Brookland
Address: 3126 12th St NE
Washington, DC 20017
Phone: (202) 636-0050

#66
Rosario
Cuisines: Italian, Cocktail Bars, Wine Bars
Average price: Modest
Area: Adams Morgan
Address: 2435 18th St NW
Washington, DC 20009
Phone: (202) 791-0298

#67
Sfoglina
Cuisines: Italian
Average price: Expensive
Area: Van Ness/Forest Hills
Address: 4445 Connecticut Ave NW
Washington, DC 20008
Phone: (202) 450-1312

#68
Lavagna
Cuisines: Italian
Average price: Modest
Area: Capitol Hill
Address: 539 8th St SE
Washington, DC 20003
Phone: (202) 546-5006

#69
Zannchi
Cuisines: Korean, Barbeque, Soup
Average price: Modest
Area: Georgetown
Address: 1529 Wisconsin Ave NW
Washington, DC 20007
Phone: (202) 621-9162

#70
Huacatay Peruvian Chicken
Cuisines: Peruvian, Chicken Shop
Average price: Inexpensive
Area: Edgewood
Address: 2314 4th St NE
Washington, DC 20002
Phone: (202) 795-9940

#71
Mola
Cuisines: Spanish
Average price: Modest
Area: Mount Pleasant
Address: 3155 Mount Pleasant St NW
Washington, DC 20010
Phone: (202) 849-3247

#72
Tartufo
Cuisines: Italian
Average price: Modest
Area: Tenleytown
Address: 4910 Wisconsin Ave NW
Washington, DC 20016
Phone: (202) 243-1078

#73
Eatbar
Cuisines: Bars, American, Burgers
Average price: Modest
Area: Capitol Hill
Address: 415 8th St SE
Washington, DC 20003
Phone: (202) 847-4827

#74
The Passenger
Cuisines: Bars, American
Average price: Modest
Area: Shaw
Address: 1539 7th St NW
Washington, DC 20001
Phone: (202) 853-3588

#75
Yafa Grille
Cuisines: Middle Eastern, Mediterranean
Average price: Inexpensive
Area: Downtown
Address: 1400 I St NW
Washington, DC 20005
Phone: (202) 733-1544

#76
The Bird
Cuisines: American, Breakfast & Brunch
Average price: Modest
Area: Shaw, Downtown
Address: 1337 11th St NW
Washington, DC 20001
Phone: (202) 518-3609

#77
Let's Mix! Bibija!
Cuisines: Asian Fusion, Korean
Average price: Modest
Area: Capitol Hill
Address: 209 Pennsylvania Ave SE
Washington, DC 20003
Phone: (202) 544-3049

#78
CRISP Kitchen + Bar
Cuisines: Burgers, Bars, Chicken Wings
Average price: Modest
Area: Bloomingdale
Address: 1837 1st St NW
Washington, DC 20001
Phone: (202) 853-9115

#79
District Kitchen
Cuisines: American
Average price: Modest
Area: Woodley Park
Address: 2606 Connecticut Ave NW
Washington, DC 20008
Phone: (202) 238-9408

#80
Acadiana
Cuisines: Cajun/Creole,
Cocktail Bars, American
Average price: Expensive
Area: Downtown
Address: 901 New York Ave NW
Washington, DC 20001
Phone: (202) 408-8848

#81
Shanghai Lounge
Cuisines: Chinese, Asian Fusion, Bars
Average price: Modest
Area: Georgetown
Address: 1734 Wisconsin Ave NW
Washington, DC 20007
Phone: (202) 338-1588

#82
Tico DC
Cuisines: Mexican, Tapas, Latin American
Average price: Modest
Area: U Street Corridor
Address: 1926 14th St NW
Washington, DC 20009
Phone: (202) 319-1400

#83
All Purpose Pizzeria
Cuisines: Pizza, Italian, Wine Bars
Average price: Modest
Area: Shaw, Downtown
Address: 1250 9th St NW
Washington, DC 20001
Phone: (202) 849-6174

#84
Granville Moore's
Cuisines: American, Belgian, Gastropubs
Average price: Modest
Area: H Street Corridor/Atlas District
Address: 1238 H St NE
Washington, DC 20002
Phone: (202) 399-2546

#85
The Haymaker Bar
Cuisines: American, Gastropubs
Average price: Modest
Area: H Street Corridor/Atlas District
Address: 1015 H St NE
Washington, DC 20002
Phone: (202) 388-4020

#86
Estadio
Cuisines: Spanish, Tapas/Small Plates
Average price: Expensive
Area: Logan Circle
Address: 1520 14th St NW
Washington, DC 20005
Phone: (202) 319-1404

#87
Luke's Lobster Georgetown
Cuisines: Seafood
Average price: Modest
Area: Georgetown
Address: 1211 Potomac St NW
Washington, DC 20007
Phone: (202) 333-4863

#88
Steel Plate
Cuisines: Cocktail Bars, Comfort Food
Average price: Modest
Area: Brookland
Address: 3523 12th St NE
Washington, DC 20017
Phone: (202) 290-2310

#89
Donburi
Cuisines: Japanese
Average price: Modest
Area: Adams Morgan
Address: 2438 18th N W
Washington, DC 20009
Phone: (202) 629-1047

#90
Boqueria
Cuisines: Tapas Bars, Spanish
Average price: Expensive
Area: Downtown
Address: 1837 M St NW
Washington, DC 20036
Phone: (202) 558-9545

#91
Agora
Cuisines: Mediterranean, Turkish, Lebanese
Average price: Modest
Area: Dupont Circle
Address: 1527 17th St NW
Washington, DC 20036
Phone: (202) 332-6767

#92
OKI Bowl At Georgetown
Cuisines: Ramen
Average price: Modest
Area: Georgetown
Address: 1608 Wisconsin Ave NW
Washington, DC 20007
Phone: (202) 944-8660

#93
Lincoln
Cuisines: American, Bars,
Tapas/Small Plates
Average price: Modest
Area: Downtown
Address: 1110 Vermont Ave NW
Washington, DC 20005
Phone: (202) 386-9200

#94
Sotto
Cuisines: Cocktail Bars, Jazz & Blues,
Barbeque
Average price: Modest
Area: Logan Circle
Address: 1610 14th St NW
Washington, DC 20009
Phone: (202) 545-3459

#95
The Red Hen
Cuisines: Italian, Desserts, Cocktail Bars
Average price: Expensive
Area: Bloomingdale
Address: 1822 1st St NW
Washington, DC 20002
Phone: (202) 525-3021

#96
The Prospect
Cuisines: Sports Bars, American, Gastropubs
Average price: Modest
Area: U Street Corridor
Address: 1214 U St NW
Washington, DC 20009
Phone: (202) 450-4130

#97
Far East Taco Grille
Cuisines: Mexican, Asian Fusion
Average price: Inexpensive
Area: Capitol Hill
Address: 409 15th St NE
Washington, DC 20002
Phone: (202) 601-4346

#98
Hank's Oyster Bar
Cuisines: Seafood, Bars, American
Average price: Modest
Area: Dupont Circle
Address: 1624 Q St NW
Washington, DC 20009
Phone: (202) 462-4265

#99
The Sovereign
Cuisines: Belgian, Beer Bar
Average price: Modest
Area: Georgetown
Address: 1206 Wisconsin Ave NW
Washington, DC 20007
Phone: (202) 774-5875

#100
Smith Public Trust
Cuisines: American, Pubs
Average price: Modest
Area: Brookland
Address: 3514 12th St NE
Washington, DC 20017
Phone: (202) 733-5834

#101
Arepa House DC
Cuisines: Venezuelan
Average price: Inexpensive
Area: Adams Morgan
Address: 2120 18th St NW
Washington, DC 20009
Phone: (202) 588-0511

#102
Tortino Restaurant
Cuisines: Italian
Average price: Modest
Area: Logan Circle, Downtown
Address: 1228 11th St NW
Washington, DC 20001
Phone: (202) 312-5570

#103
District Commons
Cuisines: Beer Bar, Cocktail Bars, American
Average price: Modest
Area: Foggy Bottom, Downtown
Address: 2200 Pennsylvania Ave NW
Washington, DC 20037
Phone: (202) 587-8277

#104
Flavio Restaurant
Cuisines: Italian, Wine Bars
Average price: Modest
Area: Georgetown
Address: 1073 31st St NW
Washington, DC 20007
Phone: (202) 965-6666

#105
Capitol Hill Crab Cakes
Cuisines: American, Cupcakes
Average price: Modest
Area: Anacostia
Address: 1243 Good Hope Rd SE
Washington, DC 20020
Phone: (202) 678-5000

#106
Macintyre's
Cuisines: Sandwiches, Pubs, Burgers
Average price: Modest
Area: Woodley Park
Address: 2621 Connecticut Ave NW
Washington, DC 20008
Phone: (202) 506-3427

#107
CAVA
Cuisines: Mediterranean
Average price: Modest
Area: Chinatown
Address: 707 H St NW
Washington, DC 20001
Phone: (202) 719-0111

#108
Rasika
Cuisines: Indian
Average price: Expensive
Area: Penn Quarter
Address: 633 D St NW
Washington, DC 20004
Phone: (202) 637-1222

#109
DC Noodles
Cuisines: Noodles
Average price: Modest
Area: U Street Corridor
Address: 1412 U St NW
Washington, DC 20009
Phone: (202) 232-8424

#110
Good Stuff Eatery
Cuisines: American, Burgers
Average price: Modest
Area: Georgetown
Address: 3291 M St NW
Washington, DC 20007
Phone: (202) 337-4663

#111
St. Arnold's
Cuisines: Belgian, Pubs, American
Average price: Modest
Area: Dupont Circle, Downtown
Address: 1827 Jefferson Pl NW
Washington, DC 20036
Phone: (202) 833-1321

#112
Busboys And Poets - 14th And V
Cuisines: Breakfast & Brunch, American
Average price: Modest
Area: U Street Corridor
Address: 2021 14th St NW
Washington, DC 20009
Phone: (202) 387-7638

#113
Barcelona Wine Bar
Cuisines: Tapas/Small Plates,
Wine Bars, Spanish
Average price: Modest
Area: Logan Circle
Address: 1622 14th St NW
Washington, DC 20005
Phone: (202) 588-5500

#114
Thai Pad
Cuisines: Thai
Average price: Modest
Area: Van Ness/Forest Hills
Address: 4481 Connecticut Ave NW
Washington, DC 20008
Phone: (202) 244-8424

#115
The Airedale
Cuisines: Gastropubs
Average price: Modest
Area: Columbia Heights
Address: 3605 14th St
Washington, DC 20010
Phone: (202) 722-1212

#116
Matchbox - Chinatown
Cuisines: Pizza, American
Average price: Modest
Area: Chinatown
Address: 713 H St NW
Washington, DC 20001
Phone: (202) 289-4441

#117
Nazca Mochica
Cuisines: Peruvian, Lounges
Average price: Modest
Area: Dupont Circle, Downtown
Address: 1633 P St NW
Washington, DC 20036
Phone: (202) 733-3170

#118
The Source
Cuisines: Asian Fusion, Dim Sum, Japanese
Average price: Expensive
Area: Penn Quarter
Address: 575 Pennsylvania Ave NW
Washington, DC 20565
Phone: (202) 637-6100

#119
Maple
Cuisines: Wine Bars, Italian
Average price: Modest
Area: Columbia Heights
Address: 3418 11th St NW
Washington, DC 20010
Phone: (202) 588-7442

#120
Falafel Inc
Cuisines: Falafel, Vegetarian
Average price: Inexpensive
Area: Georgetown
Address: 1210 Potomac St NW
Washington, DC 20007
Phone: (202) 333-4265

#121
El Rinconcito Cafe
Cuisines: Salvadoran, Mexican
Average price: Inexpensive
Area: Downtown
Address: 1129 11th St NW
Washington, DC 20001
Phone: (202) 789-4110

#122
Mi Cuba Cafe
Cuisines: Cuban, Latin American, Caribbean
Average price: Modest
Area: Columbia Heights
Address: 1424 Park Rd NW
Washington, DC 20010
Phone: (202) 813-3489

#123
Nagomi Izakaya
Cuisines: Ramen, Izakaya
Average price: Modest
Area: Downtown
Address: 1990 M St NW
Washington, DC 20036
Phone: (202) 525-4016

#124
Sudhouse
Cuisines: Gastropubs,
Sports Bars, Venues & Event Spaces
Average price: Modest
Area: U Street Corridor
Address: 1340 U St NW
Washington, DC 20009
Phone: (202) 525-4188

#125
Benitos Place
Cuisines: Latin American, Honduran
Average price: Modest
Area: Shaw, Downtown
Address: 1431 11th St NW
Washington, DC 20001
Phone: (202) 299-0977

#126
Osteria Morini
Cuisines: Italian
Average price: Expensive
Area: Navy Yard
Address: 301 Water St SE
Washington, DC 20003
Phone: (202) 484-0660

#127
Ezme Restaurant & Wine Bar
Cuisines: Turkish, Mediterranean,
Tapas/Small Plates
Average price: Modest
Area: Dupont Circle, Downtown
Address: 2016 P St NW
Washington, DC 20036
Phone: (202) 223-4303

#128
The Salt Line
Cuisines: Seafood, American
Average price: Modest
Area: Navy Yard
Address: 79 Potomac Ave SE
Washington, DC 20003
Phone: (202) 506-2368

#129
Mythology
Cuisines: American, Lounges
Average price: Modest
Area: H Street Corridor/Atlas District
Address: 816 H St NE
Washington, DC 20002
Phone: (202) 847-0098

#130
1789 Restaurant
Cuisines: American, Ice Cream
Average price: Exclusive
Area: Georgetown
Address: 1226 36th St NW
Washington, DC 20007
Phone: (202) 965-1789

#131
**Joe's Seafood, Prime
Steak & Stone Crab**
Cuisines: Seafood, Steakhouses
Average price: Expensive
Area: Downtown
Address: 750 15th St NW
Washington, DC 20005
Phone: (202) 489-0140

#132
El Sol Restaurant & Tequileria
Cuisines: Mexican, Beer Bar
Average price: Modest
Area: Shaw, Downtown
Address: 1227 11th St NW
Washington, DC 20001
Phone: (202) 815-4789

#133
GCDC Grilled Cheese Bar
Cuisines: American, Comfort Food
Average price: Modest
Area: Downtown
Address: 1730 Pennsylvania Ave NW
Washington, DC 20006
Phone: (202) 393-4232

#134
Third Eye Tavern
Cuisines: American, Pubs
Average price: Inexpensive
Area: Dupont Circle
Address: 1723 Connecticut Ave NW
Washington, DC 20009
Phone: (202) 588-0507

#135
Tulips
Cuisines: Bars, American
Average price: Expensive
Area: Dupont Circle, Downtown
Address: 1207 19th St NW
Washington, DC 20036
Phone: (202) 420-9666

#136
El Chalán
Cuisines: Peruvian
Average price: Modest
Area: Downtown
Address: 1924 I St NW
Washington, DC 20006
Phone: (202) 293-2765

#137
The Bespoke Kitchen
Cuisines: American
Average price: Exclusive
Area: Brookland
Address: 2212 Rhode Island Ave NE
Washington, DC 20018
Phone: (202) 733-3106

#138
Ruta Del Vino
Cuisines: Wine Bars, Latin American
Average price: Modest
Area: Petworth
Address: 800 Upshur St NW
Washington, DC 20011
Phone: (202) 248-4469

#139
Roti Modern Mediterranean
Cuisines: Mediterranean
Average price: Inexpensive
Area: Foggy Bottom
Address: 2221 I St NW
Washington, DC 20052
Phone: (202) 499-2095

#140
Brasserie Beck
Cuisines: Belgian, Modern European
Average price: Expensive
Area: Downtown
Address: 1101 K St NW
Washington, DC 20005
Phone: (202) 408-1717

#141
Tabard Inn Restaurant
Cuisines: American,
Breakfast & Brunch, Burgers
Average price: Modest
Area: Dupont Circle, Downtown
Address: 1739 N St NW
Washington, DC 20036
Phone: (202) 331-8528

#142
Salt & Pepper
Cuisines: Southern, American
Average price: Modest
Area: Palisades
Address: 5125 Macarthur Blvd
Washington, DC 20016
Phone: (202) 364-5125

#143
Thai Chef Street Food
Cuisines: Thai
Average price: Modest
Area: Dupont Circle
Address: 1712 Connecticut Ave NW
Washington, DC 20009
Phone: (202) 234-5698

#144
Etto
Cuisines: Bars, Italian, Pizza
Average price: Modest
Area: Logan Circle
Address: 1541 14th St NW
Washington, DC 20005
Phone: (202) 232-0920

#145
Mintwood Place
Cuisines: American, French, Bars
Average price: Expensive
Area: Adams Morgan
Address: 1813 Columbia Rd NW
Washington, DC 20009
Phone: (202) 234-6732

#146
Penn Grill
Cuisines: Sandwiches, Mongolian, Korean
Average price: Inexpensive
Area: Downtown
Address: 825 20th St NW
Washington, DC 20006
Phone: (202) 296-0620

#147
Taqueria & Rosticeria Fresca
Cuisines: Mexican, Latin American
Average price: Inexpensive
Area: H Street Corridor/Atlas District
Address: 701 H St NE
Washington, DC 20002
Phone: (202) 544-1579

#148
Moreland's Tavern
Cuisines: American, Bars
Average price: Modest
Area: Brightwood
Address: 5501 14th St NW
Washington, DC 20011
Phone: (202) 248-0491

#149
Momiji
Cuisines: Japanese, Sushi Bars, Bars
Average price: Modest
Area: Chinatown
Address: 505 H St NW
Washington, DC 20001
Phone: (202) 408-8110

#150
Bozzelli's
Cuisines: Pizza, Italian, Sandwiches
Average price: Inexpensive
Area: Downtown
Address: 1025 Vermont Ave NW
Washington, DC 20005
Phone: (202) 347-6810

#151
Off The Record
Cuisines: Bars, American
Average price: Expensive
Area: Downtown
Address: 800 16th St NW
Washington, DC 20006
Phone: (202) 638-6600

#152
Mama Ayesha's
Cuisines: Middle Eastern,
Mediterranean, Syrian
Average price: Modest
Area: Adams Morgan
Address: 1967 Calvert St NW
Washington, DC 20009
Phone: (202) 232-5431

#153
Umi Japanese Cuisine
Cuisines: Sushi Bars, Japanese
Average price: Modest
Area: Woodley Park
Address: 2625 Connecticut Ave
Washington, DC 20008
Phone: (202) 332-3636

#154
Charcoal Town Shawarma
Cuisines: Mediterranean,
Middle Eastern, Kebab
Average price: Inexpensive
Area: U Street Corridor
Address: 2019 11th St NW
Washington, DC 20001
Phone: (202) 232-2330

#155
RASA
Cuisines: Indian
Average price: Modest
Area: Navy Yard
Address: 1247 First St SE
Washington, DC 20003
Phone: (202) 804-5678

#156
Heat Da Spot
Cuisines: Cafes
Average price: Inexpensive
Area: Park View
Address: 3213 Georgia Ave NW
Washington, DC 20010
Phone: (202) 836-4719

#157
The Good Silver
Cuisines: Cocktail Bars, American
Average price: Modest
Area: Columbia Heights
Address: 3410 11th St NW
Washington, DC 20010
Phone: (202) 505-4522

#158
Timber Pizza Company
Cuisines: Pizza
Average price: Modest
Area: Petworth
Address: 809 Upshur St NW
Washington, DC 20011
Phone: (202) 853-9746

#159
Grillfish DC
Cuisines: Seafood, American
Average price: Modest
Area: Downtown
Address: 1200 New Hampshire Ave NW
Washington, DC 20036
Phone: (202) 331-7310

#160
CAVA
Cuisines: Mediterranean
Average price: Inexpensive
Area: Dupont Circle, Downtown
Address: 1222 Connecticut Ave NW
Washington, DC 20036
Phone: (202) 370-6636

#161
Nando's Peri-Peri
Cuisines: Portuguese,
South African, Chicken Shop
Average price: Modest
Area: Chinatown
Address: 819 7th St NW
Washington, DC 20001
Phone: (202) 898-1225

#162
Scarlet Oak
Cuisines: American
Average price: Modest
Area: Navy Yard
Address: 909 New Jersey Ave SE
Washington, DC 20003
Phone: (202) 780-0140

#163
China Boy
Cuisines: Chinese
Average price: Inexpensive
Area: Chinatown
Address: 815 6th St NW
Washington, DC 20001
Phone: (202) 371-1661

#164
Bul
Cuisines: Korean, Bars
Average price: Modest
Area: Adams Morgan
Address: 2431 18th St NW
Washington, DC 20009
Phone: (202) 733-3921

#165
Soi 38
Cuisines: Thai
Average price: Modest
Area: Downtown
Address: 2101 L St NW
Washington, DC 20037
Phone: (202) 558-9215

#166
Pow Pow
Cuisines: Asian Fusion, Vegetarian, Vegan
Average price: Modest
Area: H Street Corridor/Atlas District
Address: 1253 H St NE
Washington, DC 20002
Phone: (202) 399-1364

#167
Chicken + Whiskey
Cuisines: Venezuelan, Peruvian, Sandwiches
Average price: Modest
Area: Logan Circle
Address: 1738 14th St NW
Washington, DC 20009
Phone: (202) 667-2456

#168
Bluefin Sushi
Cuisines: Sushi Bars, Japanese
Average price: Modest
Area: Georgetown
Address: 3073 Canal St NW
Washington, DC 20007
Phone: (202) 333-6774

#169
Corduroy
Cuisines: American
Average price: Expensive
Area: Downtown
Address: 1122 9th St NW
Washington, DC 20001
Phone: (202) 589-0699

#170
Medium Rare
Cuisines: Steakhouses, American, Desserts
Average price: Modest
Area: Cleveland Park
Address: 3500 Connecticut Ave NW
Washington, DC 20008
Phone: (202) 237-1432

#171
Curry & Pie
Cuisines: Indian, Pizza, Asian Fusion
Average price: Modest
Area: Georgetown
Address: 1204 34th St NW
Washington, DC 20007
Phone: (202) 333-4369

#172
Blue 44 Restaurant & Bar
Cuisines: American
Average price: Modest
Area: Chevy Chase
Address: 5507 Connecticut Ave NW
Washington, DC 20015
Phone: (202) 362-2583

#173
Aroi Fine Thai & Japanese Cuisine
Cuisines: Sushi Bars, Thai, Asian Fusion
Average price: Modest
Area: Bloomingdale
Address: 1832 1st St NW
Washington, DC 20001
Phone: (202) 652-0642

#174
District Rico
Cuisines: Peruvian
Average price: Inexpensive
Area: Noma
Address: 91 H St
Washington, DC 20001
Phone: (202) 842-5007

#175
Garden Cafe
Cuisines: American, Cafes
Average price: Modest
Area: Foggy Bottom
Address: 2117 E St NW
Washington, DC 20037
Phone: (202) 861-0331

#176
Malbec Restaurant
Cuisines: Argentine
Average price: Modest
Area: Dupont Circle
Address: 1633 17th St NW
Washington, DC 20009
Phone: (202) 232-0437

#177
Catch 15
Cuisines: Bars, Italian, Seafood
Average price: Modest
Area: Downtown
Address: 1518 K St NW
Washington, DC 20005
Phone: (202) 969-2858

#178
I-Thai Restaurant & Sushi Bar
Cuisines: Thai, Sushi Bars
Average price: Modest
Area: Georgetown
Address: 3003 M St NW
Washington, DC 20007
Phone: (202) 580-8852

#179
Ana At District Winery
Cuisines: American, Bars
Average price: Expensive
Area: Navy Yard
Address: 385 Water St SE
Washington, DC 20003
Phone: (202) 484-9210

#180
Arroz
Cuisines: Spanish, Moroccan, Cocktail Bars
Average price: Expensive
Area: Downtown
Address: 901 Massachusetts Ave NW
Washington, DC 20001
Phone: (202) 869-3300

#181
Brick Lane
Cuisines: Breakfast & Brunch, American
Average price: Modest
Area: Dupont Circle
Address: 1636 17th St NW
Washington, DC 20009
Phone: (202) 525-5309

#182
Rice Bar
Cuisines: Korean, Delis
Average price: Modest
Area: Downtown
Address: 1020 19th St NW
Washington, DC 20036
Phone: (202) 429-1701

#183
Las Placitas
Cuisines: Salvadoran, Mexican
Average price: Modest
Area: Navy Yard
Address: 1100 8th St SE
Washington, DC 20003
Phone: (202) 543-3700

#184
Torai
Cuisines: Sushi Bars, Pan Asian
Average price: Modest
Area: Capitol Hill
Address: 751 8th St SE
Washington, DC 20003
Phone: (202) 525-2053

#185
Un Je Ne Sais Quoi
Cuisines: Desserts, Cafes, Bakeries
Average price: Inexpensive
Area: Dupont Circle, Downtown
Address: 1361 Connecticut Ave NW
Washington, DC 20036
Phone: (202) 721-0099

#186
Barmini By José Andrés
Cuisines: American, Cocktail Bars
Average price: Expensive
Area: Penn Quarter
Address: 501 9th St NW
Washington, DC 20004
Phone: (202) 393-4451

#187
Seoulspice
Cuisines: Korean, Comfort Food, Gluten-Free
Average price: Inexpensive
Area: Tenleytown
Address: 4600 Wisconsin Ave NW
Washington, DC 20016
Phone: (202) 792-8879

#188
Otello
Cuisines: Italian
Average price: Modest
Area: Dupont Circle, Downtown
Address: 1329 Connecticut Ave NW
Washington, DC 20036
Phone: (202) 429-0209

#189
Panas Empanadas
Cuisines: Latin American, Empanadas
Average price: Inexpensive
Area: Dupont Circle, Downtown
Address: 2029 P St NW
Washington, DC 20036
Phone: (202) 223-2964

#190
Sushi Taro
Cuisines: Sushi Bars, Japanese
Average price: Exclusive
Area: Dupont Circle, Downtown
Address: 1503 17th St NW
Washington, DC 20036
Phone: (202) 462-8999

#191
Duke's Grocery
Cuisines: Bars, Sandwiches, Salad
Average price: Modest
Area: Dupont Circle
Address: 1513 17th St NW
Washington, DC 20036
Phone: (202) 733-5623

#192
BKK Cookshop
Cuisines: Thai
Average price: Modest
Area: Shaw
Address: 1700 New Jersey Ave NW
Washington, DC 20001
Phone: (202) 791-0592

#193
Po Boy Jim
Cuisines: Cajun/Creole, Bars, American
Average price: Modest
Area: H Street Corridor/Atlas District
Address: 709 H St NE
Washington, DC 20002
Phone: (202) 621-7071

#194
Komi
Cuisines: Greek
Average price: Exclusive
Area: Dupont Circle
Address: 1509 17th St NW
Washington, DC 20036
Phone: (202) 332-9200

#195
Prequel
Cuisines: Wine Bars, Burgers, Hot Dogs
Average price: Modest
Area: Downtown
Address: 919 19th St NW
Washington, DC 20005
Phone: (202) 510-9917

#196
14th St Cafe Asian Bistro
Cuisines: Chinese
Average price: Modest
Area: Logan Circle, Downtown
Address: 1416 14th St NW
Washington, DC 20005
Phone: (202) 588-0695

#197
Macon Bistro & Larder
Cuisines: Southern, Wine Bars, Cocktail Bars
Average price: Modest
Area: Chevy Chase
Address: 5520 Connecticut Ave NW
Washington, DC 20015
Phone: (202) 248-7807

#198
Kabob Square
Cuisines: Food Trucks, Mediterranean
Average price: Inexpensive
Area: Federal Triangle
Address: 1416 Constitution Ave NW
Washington, DC 20004
Phone: (703) 401-0805

#199
Siam House Thai Restaurant
Cuisines: Thai
Average price: Modest
Area: Cleveland Park
Address: 3520 Connecticut Ave NW
Washington, DC 20008
Phone: (202) 363-7802

#200
Triple B Fresh
Cuisines: Korean
Average price: Inexpensive
Area: Dupont Circle
Address: 1506 19th St NW
Washington, DC 20036
Phone: (202) 232-2338

#201
Cava Mezze
Cuisines: Greek, Mediterranean, Seafood
Average price: Modest
Area: Capitol Hill
Address: 527 8th St SE
Washington, DC 20003
Phone: (202) 543-9090

#202
Georgia Brown's
Cuisines: Southern, Soul Food, Cocktail Bars
Average price: Expensive
Area: Downtown
Address: 950 15th St NW
Washington, DC 20005
Phone: (202) 393-4499

#203
Amsterdam Falafelshop
Cuisines: Vegetarian, Middle Eastern, Falafel
Average price: Inexpensive
Area: Adams Morgan
Address: 2425 18th St NW
Washington, DC 20009
Phone: (202) 234-1969

#204
The Italians Kitchen
Cuisines: Pizza, Italian
Average price: Modest
Area: Woodley Park
Address: 2608 Connecticut Ave NW
Washington, DC 20008
Phone: (202) 939-2979

#205
Provision No 14
Cuisines: Cocktail Bars, American
Average price: Modest
Area: U Street Corridor
Address: 2100 14th St NW
Washington, DC 20009
Phone: (202) 827-4530

#206
Chaia
Cuisines: Vegetarian, Tacos
Average price: Modest
Area: Georgetown
Address: 3207 Grace St NW
Washington, DC 20007
Phone: (202) 333-5222

#207
DC Harvest
Cuisines: American, Bars
Average price: Modest
Area: H Street Corridor/Atlas District
Address: 517 H St NE
Washington, DC 20002
Phone: (202) 629-3296

#208
Casa Luca
Cuisines: Italian
Average price: Expensive
Area: Downtown
Address: 1099 New York Ave NW
Washington, DC 20001
Phone: (202) 628-1099

#209
Eat The Rich
Cuisines: Seafood, Cocktail Bars
Average price: Modest
Area: Shaw
Address: 1839 7th St NW
Washington, DC 20001
Phone: (202) 316-9396

#210
Zeitoun
Cuisines: Mediterranean, Italian, Sandwiches
Average price: Inexpensive
Area: Foggy Bottom
Address: 2554 Virginia Ave NW
Washington, DC 20037
Phone: (202) 560-5372

#211
Right Spot Restaurant & Bar
Cuisines: Bars, French, American
Average price: Modest
Area: Shaw
Address: 1917 9th St NW
Washington, DC 20001
Phone: (202) 455-4498

#212
The Commodore
Public House And Kitchen
Cuisines: American, Bars
Average price: Modest
Area: Logan Circle, Downtown
Address: 1100 P St NW
Washington, DC 20005
Phone: (202) 234-6870

#213
Hawthorne
Cuisines: Bars, American
Average price: Modest
Area: U Street Corridor
Address: 1336 U St NW
Washington, DC 20009
Phone: (202) 853-9194

#214
The Big Stick
Cuisines: Bars, American, Desserts
Average price: Modest
Area: Navy Yard
Address: 20 M St SE
Washington, DC 20003
Phone: (202) 750-7724

#215
Los Hermanos
Cuisines: Dominican
Average price: Inexpensive
Area: Columbia Heights
Address: 1426 Park Rd NW
Washington, DC 20010
Phone: (202) 483-8235

#216
Birch & Barley
Cuisines: American, Breakfast & Brunch
Average price: Expensive
Area: Logan Circle, Downtown
Address: 1337 14th St NW
Washington, DC 20005
Phone: (202) 567-2576

#217
Nando's Peri-Peri
Cuisines: Portuguese,
South African, Chicken Shop
Average price: Modest
Area: Dupont Circle, Downtown
Address: 1210 18th St NW
Washington, DC 20036
Phone: (202) 621-8600

#218
Hando Medo
Cuisines: Sushi Bars, Japanese
Average price: Modest
Area: Logan Circle, Downtown
Address: 1315 14th St NW
Washington, DC 20005
Phone: (202) 450-5882

#219
Via Umbria
Cuisines: Italian, Beer,
Wine & Spirits, Cheese Shops
Average price: Modest
Area: Georgetown
Address: 1525 Wisconsin Ave NW
Washington, DC 20007
Phone: (202) 559-7359

#220
Bistro Aracosia
Cuisines: Afghan
Average price: Expensive
Area: Palisades
Address: 5100 Macarthur Blvd
Washington, DC 20016
Phone: (202) 363-0400

#221
Blacksalt
Cuisines: Seafood, American
Average price: Expensive
Area: Palisades
Address: 4883 Macarthur Blvd NW
Washington, DC 20007
Phone: (202) 342-9101

#222
Rasika West End
Cuisines: Indian
Average price: Expensive
Area: West End, Downtown
Address: 1190 New Hampshire Ave NW
Washington, DC 20037
Phone: (202) 466-2500

#223
Espita Mezcaleria
Cuisines: Mexican, Bars
Average price: Modest
Area: Shaw, Downtown
Address: 1250 9th St NW
Washington, DC 20001
Phone: (202) 621-9695

#224
BLT Steak
Cuisines: Steakhouses
Average price: Exclusive
Area: Downtown
Address: 1625 I St NW
Washington, DC 20006
Phone: (202) 689-8999

#225
Tryst
Cuisines: Lounges, American
Average price: Modest
Area: Adams Morgan
Address: 2459 18th St NW
Washington, DC 20009
Phone: (202) 232-5500

#226
Nando's Peri-Peri
Cuisines: Chicken Shop,
Portuguese, South African
Average price: Modest
Area: Woodley Park
Address: 2631 Connecticut Ave
Washington, DC 20008
Phone: (202) 204-1251

#227
Pho Anh Dao
Cuisines: Vietnamese
Average price: Modest
Area: Dupont Circle
Address: 1915 18th St NW
Washington, DC 20009
Phone: (202) 232-1800

#228
BIBIBOP Asian Grill
Cuisines: Korean, Asian Fusion, Salad
Average price: Inexpensive
Area: Georgetown
Address: 2805 M St NW
Washington, DC 20007
Phone: (202) 650-7219

#229
Las Canteras
Cuisines: Latin American, Peruvian
Average price: Modest
Area: Adams Morgan
Address: 2307 18th St NW
Washington, DC 20009
Phone: (202) 265-1780

#230
CAVA
Cuisines: Mediterranean
Average price: Inexpensive
Area: Shaw
Address: 1921 8th Street NW
Washington, DC 20001
Phone: (949) 200-7998

#231
Bareburger
Cuisines: American, Burgers, Salad
Average price: Modest
Area: Dupont Circle
Address: 1647 Connecticut Ave NW
Washington, DC 20009
Phone: (202) 888-4582

#232
Dolan Uyghur Restaurant
Cuisines: Asian Fusion, Middle Eastern, Halal
Average price: Modest
Area: Cleveland Park
Address: 3518 Connecticut Ave NW
Washington, DC 20008
Phone: (202) 686-3941

#233
Indigo
Cuisines: Indian
Average price: Modest
Area: H Street Corridor/Atlas District
Address: 243 K St NE
Washington, DC 20002
Phone: (202) 544-4777

#234
Room 11
Cuisines: Wine Bars, American, Cocktail Bars
Average price: Modest
Area: Columbia Heights
Address: 3234 11th St NW
Washington, DC 20010
Phone: (202) 332-3234

#235
Wicked Waffle
Cuisines: Breakfast & Brunch,
Sandwiches, Gluten-Free
Average price: Inexpensive
Area: Downtown
Address: 1712 I St NW
Washington, DC 20006
Phone: (202) 944-2700

#236
Pizzeria Paradiso
Cuisines: Pizza, Beer Bar
Average price: Modest
Area: Dupont Circle, Downtown
Address: 2003 P St NW
Washington, DC 20036
Phone: (202) 223-1245

#237
Tilt
Cuisines: Bars, American
Average price: Modest
Area: Logan Circle
Address: 1612 14th St NW
Washington, DC 20005
Phone: (202) 319-1612

#238
Iron Gate
Cuisines: American, Greek
Average price: Expensive
Area: Downtown, Dupont Circle
Address: 1734 N St NW
Washington, DC 20036
Phone: (202) 524-5202

#239
Fiola
Cuisines: Italian
Average price: Exclusive
Area: Penn Quarter
Address: 601 Pennsylvania Ave NW
Washington, DC 20004
Phone: (202) 628-2888

#240
Buredo
Cuisines: Sushi Bars,
Asian Fusion, Fast Food
Average price: Modest
Area: Downtown
Address: 825 14th St NW
Washington, DC 20005
Phone: (202) 289-0033

#241
Shanghai Tokyo Cafe
Cuisines: Japanese, Thai, Chinese
Average price: Modest
Area: Columbia Heights
Address: 1376 Park Rd NW
Washington, DC 20010
Phone: (202) 846-7953

#242
Sushi Capitol
Cuisines: Japanese, Sushi Bars
Average price: Modest
Area: Capitol Hill
Address: 325 Pennsylvania Ave SE
Washington, DC 20003
Phone: (202) 627-0325

#243
Saigon Kitchen
Cuisines: Vietnamese
Average price: Modest
Area: Glover Park
Address: 2412 Wisconsin Ave NW
Washington, DC 20007
Phone: (202) 733-4175

#244
Dino's Grotto
Cuisines: Italian, Bars, Seafood
Average price: Modest
Area: U Street Corridor
Address: 1914 9th St NW
Washington, DC 20001
Phone: (202) 686-2966

#245
Tonic
Cuisines: American, Bars
Average price: Modest
Area: Foggy Bottom
Address: 2036 G St NW
Washington, DC 20052
Phone: (202) 296-0211

#246
Exiles Bar
Cuisines: Bars, Barbeque, Comfort Food
Average price: Modest
Area: U Street Corridor
Address: 1610 U St NW
Washington, DC 20009
Phone: (202) 232-2171

#247
Makoto Restaurant
Cuisines: Japanese
Average price: Exclusive
Area: Palisades
Address: 4822 Macarthur Blvd NW
Washington, DC 20007
Phone: (202) 298-6866

#248
Jojo Restaurant And Bar
Cuisines: Jazz & Blues, Lounges, American
Average price: Modest
Area: U Street Corridor
Address: 1518 U St NW
Washington, DC 20009
Phone: (202) 319-9350

#249
Brothers And Sisters
Cuisines: Cocktail Bars, Cafes
Average price: Expensive
Area: Adams Morgan
Address: 1770 Euclid St NW
Washington, DC 20009
Phone: (202) 864-4180

#250
BIBIBOP Asian Grill
Cuisines: Asian Fusion, Korean, Salad
Average price: Inexpensive
Area: Dupont Circle
Address: 1516 Connecticut Ave NW
Washington, DC 20036
Phone: (202) 567-1735

#251
West Wing Cafe
Cuisines: Salad, Delis
Average price: Modest
Area: West End
Address: 2400-C M St NW
Washington, DC 20037
Phone: (202) 525-4442

#252
Fare Well
Cuisines: Diners, Bakeries, Bars
Average price: Modest
Area: H Street Corridor/Atlas District
Address: 406 H St NE
Washington, DC 20002
Phone: (202) 367-9600

#253
Blackfinn Ameripub
Cuisines: Sports Bars, American, Pubs
Average price: Modest
Area: Downtown
Address: 1620 I St NW
Washington, DC 20006
Phone: (202) 429-4350

#254
The Partisan
Cuisines: American, Cocktail Bars, Wine Bars
Average price: Modest
Area: Penn Quarter
Address: 709 D St NW
Washington, DC 20004
Phone: (202) 524-5322

#255
West Wing Cafe
Cuisines: Delis, Coffee & Tea, Korean
Average price: Inexpensive
Area: Downtown
Address: 920 Massachusetts Ave NW
Washington, DC 20001
Phone: (202) 827-4081

#256
Medium Rare
Cuisines: Steakhouses, American
Average price: Modest
Area: Capitol Hill
Address: 515 8th St SE
Washington, DC 20003
Phone: (202) 601-7136

#257
Matchbox - Capitol Hill
Cuisines: Pizza, American
Average price: Modest
Area: Capitol Hill
Address: 521 8th St SE
Washington, DC 20003
Phone: (202) 548-0369

#258
Siroc Restaurant
Cuisines: Italian
Average price: Expensive
Area: Downtown
Address: 915 15th St NW
Washington, DC 20005
Phone: (202) 628-2220

#259
Sichuan Pavilion
Cuisines: Szechuan
Average price: Modest
Area: Downtown
Address: 1814 K St NW
Washington, DC 20006
Phone: (202) 466-7790

#260
Flip It LJ Diner
Cuisines: Diners
Average price: Modest
Area: Columbia Heights
Address: 1432 Park Rd
Washington, DC 20010
Phone: (202) 791-0786

#261
Thai And Pho Bistro
Cuisines: Vietnamese, Thai, Seafood
Average price: Modest
Area: Downtown
Address: 2153 P St NW
Washington, DC 20037
Phone: (202) 506-3508

#262
Hill Country Barbecue Market
Cuisines: Barbeque, Music Venues, Bars
Average price: Modest
Area: Penn Quarter
Address: 410 7th St NW
Washington, DC 20004
Phone: (202) 556-2050

#263
Buredo
Cuisines: Sushi Bars, Asian Fusion
Average price: Modest
Area: Dupont Circle, Downtown
Address: 1213 Connecticut Ave NW
Washington, DC 20036
Phone: (202) 838-6602

#264
Imm Thai On Georgia
Cuisines: Thai
Average price: Modest
Area: Brightwood
Address: 5832 Georgia Ave NW
Washington, DC 20011
Phone: (202) 291-2828

#265
Imm Thai On 9th
Cuisines: Thai
Average price: Modest
Area: Shaw, Downtown
Address: 1414 9th St NW
Washington, DC 20001
Phone: (202) 588-5810

#266
Surfside Taco Stand
Cuisines: Tex-Mex, Caribbean
Average price: Modest
Area: Dupont Circle, Downtown
Address: 1800 N St NW
Washington, DC 20036
Phone: (202) 466-1830

#267
Wingo's
Cuisines: American, Chicken Wings, Burgers
Average price: Inexpensive
Area: Georgetown
Address: 3207 O St NW
Washington, DC 20007
Phone: (202) 338-2478

#268
Bacio Pizzeria
Cuisines: Pizza, Italian
Average price: Modest
Area: Bloomingdale
Address: 81 Seaton Pl NW
Washington, DC 20001
Phone: (202) 232-2246

#269
Simply Banh Mi
Cuisines: Vietnamese, Halal
Average price: Inexpensive
Area: Georgetown
Address: 1624 Wisconsin Ave NW
Washington, DC 20007
Phone: (202) 333-5726

#270
Ted's Bulletin
Cuisines: Breakfast & Brunch,
American, Sandwiches
Average price: Modest
Area: Capitol Hill
Address: 505 8th St SE
Washington, DC 20003
Phone: (202) 544-8337

#271
Bub And Pop's
Cuisines: Sandwiches, American, Delis
Average price: Modest
Area: Dupont Circle, Downtown
Address: 1815 M St NW
Washington, DC 20036
Phone: (202) 457-1111

#272
Salumeria 2703
Cuisines: Delis, Italian
Average price: Modest
Area: Brookland
Address: 2703 12th St NE
Washington, DC 20017
Phone: (202) 699-2397

#273
P J Clarke's
Cuisines: American, Burgers, Bars
Average price: Modest
Area: Downtown
Address: 1600 K St NW
Washington, DC 20006
Phone: (202) 463-6610

#274
&Pizza
Cuisines: Pizza, Vegan, Vegetarian
Average price: Inexpensive
Area: Downtown
Address: 1400 K St NW
Washington, DC 20005
Phone: (202) 682-1503

#275
Vietnamese Chelsea Restaurant
Cuisines: Vietnamese
Average price: Modest
Area: Columbia Heights
Address: 1413 Park Rd NW
Washington, DC 20010
Phone: (202) 758-2415

#276
Ben's Chili Bowl
Cuisines: Hot Dogs, Burgers, American
Average price: Inexpensive
Area: U Street Corridor
Address: 1213 U St NW
Washington, DC 20009
Phone: (202) 667-0058

#277
Woodward Table
Cuisines: American
Average price: Modest
Area: Downtown
Address: 1426 H St NW
Washington, DC 20005
Phone: (202) 347-5353

#278
Lebanese Taverna
Cuisines: Lebanese, Mediterranean
Average price: Modest
Area: Woodley Park
Address: 2641 Connecticut Ave NW
Washington, DC 20008
Phone: (202) 265-8681

#279
Acqua Al 2
Cuisines: Italian
Average price: Expensive
Area: Capitol Hill
Address: 212 7th St SE
Washington, DC 20003
Phone: (202) 525-4375

#280
Beau Thai - Mount Pleasant
Cuisines: Thai, Bars
Average price: Modest
Area: Mount Pleasant
Address: 3162 Mt Pleasant St
Washington, DC 20010
Phone: (202) 450-5317

#281
Roti Modern Mediterranean
Cuisines: Mediterranean
Average price: Inexpensive
Area: Downtown
Address: 1747 Pennsylvania Ave NW
Washington, DC 20006
Phone: (202) 871-9342

#282
Lapis
Cuisines: Afghan, Cocktail Bars, Desserts
Average price: Modest
Area: Adams Morgan
Address: 1847 Columbia Rd NW
Washington, DC 20009
Phone: (202) 299-9630

#283
Caribbean Citations
Cuisines: Caribbean
Average price: Modest
Area: Anacostia
Address: 1208 Maple View Pl SE
Washington, DC 20020
Phone: (202) 750-8744

#284
Old Europe
Cuisines: German, Diners, Salad
Average price: Modest
Area: Glover Park
Address: 2434 Wisconsin Ave NW
Washington, DC 20007
Phone: (202) 333-7600

#285
Oyamel
Cuisines: Mexican, Tapas Bars
Average price: Modest
Area: Penn Quarter
Address: 401 7th St NW
Washington, DC 20004
Phone: (202) 628-1005

#286
Smoke & Barrel
Cuisines: Bars, American, Barbeque
Average price: Modest
Area: Adams Morgan
Address: 2471 18th St NW
Washington, DC 20009
Phone: (202) 319-9353

#287
Zorba's Cafe
Cuisines: Greek, Pizza, Mediterranean
Average price: Modest
Area: Dupont Circle
Address: 1612 20th St NW
Washington, DC 20009
Phone: (202) 387-8555

#288
Pho Viet
Cuisines: Vietnamese
Average price: Inexpensive
Area: Columbia Heights
Address: 3513 14th St NW
Washington, DC 20010
Phone: (202) 629-2839

#289
Maiwand Grill
Cuisines: Afghan
Average price: Modest
Area: Adams Morgan
Address: 1764 Columbia Rd NW
Washington, DC 20009
Phone: (202) 851-4700

#290
Good Stuff Eatery
Cuisines: Burgers
Average price: Modest
Area: Capitol Hill
Address: 303 Pennsylvania Ave SE
Washington, DC 20003
Phone: (202) 543-8222

#291
Panda Gourmet
Cuisines: Szechuan
Average price: Modest
Area: Gateway
Address: 2700 New York Ave NE
Washington, DC 20002
Phone: (202) 636-3588

#292
Astor Mediterranean
Cuisines: Mediterranean
Average price: Inexpensive
Area: Adams Morgan
Address: 1829 Columbia Rd NW
Washington, DC 20009
Phone: (202) 745-7495

#293
China Chilcano
Cuisines: Peruvian, Asian Fusion
Average price: Expensive
Area: Penn Quarter
Address: 418 7th St NW
Washington, DC 20004
Phone: (202) 783-0941

#294
Abunai Poke
Cuisines: Hawaiian, Poke
Average price: Modest
Area: Downtown
Address: 1920 L St NW
Washington, DC 20036
Phone: (202) 838-9718

#295
Red, White And Basil
Cuisines: Wine Bars, Italian,
Breakfast & Brunch
Average price: Modest
Area: Adams Morgan
Address: 1781 Florida Ave NW
Washington, DC 20009
Phone: (202) 518-7021

#296
Archipelago
Cuisines: Bars, American
Average price: Modest
Area: U Street Corridor
Address: 1201 U St NW
Washington, DC 20009
Phone: (202) 627-0794

#297
Little Red Fox
Cuisines: Cafes
Average price: Modest
Area: Chevy Chase
Address: 5035 Connecticut Ave
Washington, DC 20008
Phone: (202) 248-6346

#298
Sumah's
Cuisines: African
Average price: Modest
Area: Shaw
Address: 1727 7th St NW
Washington, DC 20001
Phone: (202) 462-7309

#299
Nopa Kitchen + Bar
Cuisines: American
Average price: Expensive
Area: Penn Quarter
Address: 800 F St NW
Washington, DC 20004
Phone: (202) 347-4667

#300
Sushi Hachi
Cuisines: Sushi Bars
Average price: Expensive
Area: Capitol Hill
Address: 735 8th St SE
Washington, DC 20003
Phone: (202) 640-1881

#301
DC Reynolds
Cuisines: American, Bars, Vegetarian
Average price: Modest
Area: Park View
Address: 3628 Georgia Ave NW
Washington, DC 20010
Phone: (202) 506-7178

#302
Kramerbooks & Afterwords Cafe
Cuisines: Bookstores, Bars, American
Average price: Modest
Area: Dupont Circle
Address: 1517 Connecticut Ave NW
Washington, DC 20036
Phone: (202) 387-1462

#303
Alfa Piehouse
Cuisines: Greek, Bakeries,
Breakfast & Brunch
Average price: Inexpensive
Area: Downtown
Address: 1750 H St NW
Washington, DC 20006
Phone: (202) 846-7122

#304
Afghan Grill
Cuisines: Middle Eastern, Afghan
Average price: Modest
Area: Woodley Park
Address: 2309 Calvert St NW
Washington, DC 20008
Phone: (202) 234-5095

#305
District Distilling Co
Cuisines: Distilleries, American
Average price: Modest
Area: U Street Corridor
Address: 1414 - 1418 U St NW
Washington, DC 20009
Phone: (202) 629-3787

#306
Obelisk
Cuisines: Italian
Average price: Exclusive
Area: Dupont Circle, Downtown
Address: 2029 P St NW
Washington, DC 20036
Phone: (202) 872-1180

#307
Arcuri
Cuisines: American, Pizza
Average price: Modest
Area: Glover Park
Address: 2400 Wisconsin Ave NW
Washington, DC 20007
Phone: (202) 827-8745

#308
Sabydee
Cuisines: Thai, Desserts, Laotian
Average price: Modest
Area: Mount Pleasant
Address: 3211 Mt Pleasant St NW
Washington, DC 20010
Phone: (202) 986-2093

#309
Matchbox - 14th Street
Cuisines: Pizza, American
Average price: Modest
Area: U Street Corridor
Address: 1901 14th St NW
Washington, DC 20009
Phone: (202) 328-0369

#310
1831 Bar & Lounge
Cuisines: Lounges, Sports Bars, American
Average price: Modest
Area: Downtown
Address: 1831 M St NW
Washington, DC 20036
Phone: (202) 223-1831

#311
Oohh's & Aahh's
Cuisines: Soul Food, Southern
Average price: Modest
Area: U Street Corridor
Address: 1005 U St NW
Washington, DC 20001
Phone: (202) 667-7142

#312
Al Tiramisu
Cuisines: Italian
Average price: Expensive
Area: Dupont Circle, Downtown
Address: 2014 P St NW
Washington, DC 20036
Phone: (202) 467-4466

#313
Cafe Deluxe
Cuisines: American
Average price: Modest
Area: West End
Address: 2201 M St NW
Washington, DC 20037
Phone: (202) 524-7815

#314
Sol Mexican Grill
Cuisines: Mexican
Average price: Modest
Area: Foggy Bottom
Address: 2121 H St NW
Washington, DC 20052
Phone: (202) 808-2625

#315
Havana Cafe
Cuisines: Cuban
Average price: Inexpensive
Area: Downtown
Address: 1825 I St NW
Washington, DC 20006
Phone: (202) 293-5303

#316
TACO-Ma Yucatan Chicken
Cuisines: Latin American
Average price: Modest
Area: Takoma
Address: 353 Cedar St NW
Washington, DC 20012
Phone: (202) 450-5933

#317
Campono
Cuisines: Pizza, Gelato, Cafes
Average price: Modest
Area: Foggy Bottom
Address: 600 New Hampshire Ave NW
Washington, DC 20037
Phone: (202) 505-4000

#318
La Jambe
Cuisines: Wine Bars, Cheese Shops,
Breakfast & Brunch
Average price: Modest
Area: Shaw
Address: 1550 7th St NW
Washington, DC 20001
Phone: (202) 627-2988

#319
RARE Steak And Seafood
Cuisines: Steakhouses,
eafood, Breakfast & Brunch
Average price: Exclusive
Area: Downtown
Address: 1595 I St NW
Washington, DC 20005
Phone: (202) 800-9994

#320
Pearl Dive Oyster Palace
Cuisines: Seafood, Breakfast & Brunch
Average price: Modest
Area: Logan Circle
Address: 1612 14th St NW
Washington, DC 20009
Phone: (202) 319-1612

#321
Petworth Citizen
Cuisines: Bars, American
Average price: Modest
Area: Petworth
Address: 829 Upshur St NW
Washington, DC 20011
Phone: (202) 722-2939

#322
El Torogoz
Cuisines: Mexican, Salvadoran
Average price: Modest
Area: Petworth
Address: 4231 9th St NW
Washington, DC 20011
Phone: (202) 722-6966

#323
Kellari Taverna
Cuisines: Greek, Seafood, Bars
Average price: Expensive
Area: Downtown
Address: 1700 K St NW
Washington, DC 20006
Phone: (202) 535-5274

#324
DC Grill Express
Cuisines: American, Burgers, Sandwiches
Average price: Modest
Area: Dupont Circle
Address: 1917 18th St NW
Washington, DC 20009
Phone: (202) 748-5154

#325
Pidzza
Cuisines: Pizza
Average price: Modest
Area: Ivy City
Address: 2000 Hecht Ave NE
Washington, DC 20002
Phone: (202) 635-0890

#326
Kotobuki
Cuisines: Sushi Bars, Japanese
Average price: Modest
Area: Palisades
Address: 4822 Macarthur Blvd NW
Washington, DC 20007
Phone: (202) 625-9080

#327
Sundevich
Cuisines: Sandwiches
Average price: Modest
Area: Shaw, Downtown
Address: 1314 9th St NW
Washington, DC 20001
Phone: (202) 319-1086

#328
The Diner
Cuisines: Diners, Bars
Average price: Modest
Area: Adams Morgan
Address: 2453 18th St NW
Washington, DC 20009
Phone: (202) 232-8800

#329
Slash Run
Cuisines: Burgers, Beer Bar,
Breakfast & Brunch
Average price: Modest
Area: Petworth
Address: 201 Upshur St NW
Washington, DC 20011
Phone: (202) 838-9929

#330
Kafe Leopold
Cuisines: American,
Austrian, Modern European
Average price: Modest
Area: Georgetown
Address: 3315 Cady's Aly NW
Washington, DC 20007
Phone: (202) 965-6005

#331
**Carmine's Italian Restaurant
Washington DC**
Cuisines: Italian, Venues & Event Spaces
Average price: Modest
Area: Penn Quarter
Address: 425 7th St NW
Washington, DC 20004
Phone: (202) 737-7770

#332
Lauriol Plaza
Cuisines: Mexican, Latin American, Spanish
Average price: Modest
Area: Dupont Circle
Address: 1835 18th St NW
Washington, DC 20009
Phone: (202) 387-0035

#333
Firefly
Cuisines: American, Breakfast & Brunch
Average price: Modest
Area: Dupont Circle, Downtown
Address: 1310 New Hampshire Ave NW
Washington, DC 20036
Phone: (202) 861-1310

#334
Mirabelle
Cuisines: French, American, Wine Bars
Average price: Exclusive
Area: Downtown
Address: 900 16th St NW
Washington, DC 20006
Phone: (202) 506-3833

#335
Wiseguy Pizza
Cuisines: Pizza
Average price: Inexpensive
Area: Foggy Bottom
Address: 2121 H St NW
Washington, DC 20052
Phone: (202) 250-5130

#336
SKWR Kabobline
Cuisines: Middle Eastern, Afghan, Halal
Average price: Inexpensive
Area: Downtown
Address: 1400 K St NW
Washington, DC 20005
Phone: (202) 682-1717

#337
City Tap House Dupont
Cuisines: Gastropubs
Average price: Modest
Area: Dupont Circle, Downtown
Address: 1250 Connecticut Ave NW
Washington, DC 20036
Phone: (202) 878-8235

#338
Uni Bistro
Cuisines: American, Cocktail Bars
Average price: Modest
Area: H Street Corridor/Atlas District
Address: 403 H St NE
Washington, DC 20002
Phone: (202) 675-2011

#339
The Queen Vic
Cuisines: Pubs, British, Fish & Chips
Average price: Modest
Area: H Street Corridor/Atlas District
Address: 1206 H St NE
Washington, DC 20002
Phone: (202) 396-2001

#340
Town Hall
Cuisines: Bars, American,
Venues & Event Spaces
Average price: Modest
Area: Glover Park
Address: 2340 Wisconsin Ave NW
Washington, DC 20007
Phone: (202) 333-5640

#341
Medaterra
Cuisines: Mediterranean
Average price: Modest
Area: Woodley Park
Address: 2614 Connecticut Ave NW
Washington, DC 20008
Phone: (202) 797-0400

#342
Bistro Cacao
Cuisines: French, Brasseries
Average price: Expensive
Area: Capitol Hill
Address: 320 Massachusetts Ave NE
Washington, DC 20002
Phone: (202) 546-4737

#343
CAVA
Cuisines: Mediterranean
Average price: Inexpensive
Area: Columbia Heights
Address: 3105 14th St NW
Washington, DC 20016
Phone: (202) 695-8100

#344
Ricks Cafe
Cuisines: Caribbean
Average price: Modest
Area: Hillcrest
Address: 3021 Naylor Rd SE
Washington, DC 20020
Phone: (202) 748-5871

#345
Minibar By José Andrés
Cuisines: American, Cocktail Bars
Average price: Exclusive
Area: Penn Quarter
Address: 855 E St NW
Washington, DC 20004
Phone: (202) 393-0812

#346
Rosa Mexicano
Cuisines: Mexican
Average price: Modest
Area: Penn Quarter
Address: 575 7th St NW
Washington, DC 20004
Phone: (202) 783-5522

#347
Hank's Oyster Bar
Cuisines: Seafood, Lounges
Average price: Modest
Area: Capitol Hill
Address: 633 Pennsylvania Ave SE
Washington, DC 20003
Phone: (202) 733-1971

#348
Fat Pete's Barbeque
Cuisines: Barbeque
Average price: Modest
Area: Cleveland Park
Address: 3407 Connecticut Ave NW
Washington, DC 20008
Phone: (202) 362-7777

#349
B Too
Cuisines: Belgian, Beer Bar
Average price: Modest
Area: Logan Circle, Downtown
Address: 1324 14th St NW
Washington, DC 20005
Phone: (202) 627-2800

#350
Le Desales
Cuisines: French
Average price: Expensive
Area: Downtown
Address: 1725 Desales St NW
Washington, DC 20036
Phone: (202) 506-6856

#351
Boundary Stone
Cuisines: American, Pubs, Sandwiches
Average price: Modest
Area: Bloomingdale
Address: 116 Rhode Island Ave NW
Washington, DC 20001
Phone: (202) 621-6635

#352
BLT Prime By David Burke
Cuisines: Steakhouses
Average price: Exclusive
Area: Federal Triangle
Address: 1100 Pennsylvania Ave NW
Washington, DC 20004
Phone: (202) 868-5100

#353
Beef N Bread
Cuisines: Delis, Sandwiches
Average price: Inexpensive
Area: Chinatown
Address: 750 6th St NW
Washington, DC 20001
Phone: (202) 393-0406

#354
The Heights Taproom
Cuisines: American
Average price: Modest
Area: Columbia Heights
Address: 3115 14th St NW
Washington, DC 20010
Phone: (202) 797-7227

#355
The Visiteur
Cuisines: Comfort Food, Beer, Wine &
Spirits, Breakfast & Brunch
Average price: Modest
Area: West End, Downtown
Address: 1221 22nd Street NW
Washington, DC 20037
Phone: (202) 872-1500

#356
Mari Vanna DC
Cuisines: Russian,
Modern European, Karaoke
Average price: Expensive
Area: Downtown
Address: 1141 Connecticut Ave NW
Washington, DC 20036
Phone: (202) 839-3067

#357
Nobu
Cuisines: Japanese, Sushi Bars
Average price: Exclusive
Area: West End
Address: 2525 M St NW
Washington, DC 20037
Phone: (202) 871-6565

#358
Bar A Vin
Cuisines: Wine Bars, French
Average price: Modest
Area: Georgetown
Address: 1035 31st St NW
Washington, DC 20007
Phone: (202) 965-2606

#359
Taqueria Del Barrio
Cuisines: Mexican
Average price: Modest
Area: Petworth
Address: 821 Upshur St NW
Washington, DC 20011
Phone: (202) 723-0200

#360
Supra
Cuisines: Middle Eastern, Bars, Georgian
Average price: Expensive
Area: Shaw, Downtown
Address: 1205 11th St Nw
Washington, DC 20001
Phone: (202) 789-1205

#361
CIRCA At Foggy Bottom
Cuisines: American, Sandwiches
Average price: Modest
Area: Foggy Bottom
Address: 2221 I St NW
Washington, DC 20037
Phone: (202) 506-5589

#362
SEI
Cuisines: Sushi Bars,
Japanese, Cocktail Bars
Average price: Expensive
Area: Penn Quarter
Address: 444 7th St NW
Washington, DC 20004
Phone: (202) 783-7007

#363
Sorriso Bistro
Cuisines: Italian, Gelato, Breakfast & Brunch
Average price: Modest
Area: Woodley Park
Address: 2311 Calvert St NW
Washington, DC 20008
Phone: (202) 803-2872

#364
Indique
Cuisines: Indian, Bars
Average price: Modest
Area: Cleveland Park
Address: 3512-14 Connecticut Ave NW
Washington, DC 20008
Phone: (202) 244-6600

#365
Bolt Burgers
Cuisines: Burgers
Average price: Modest
Area: Downtown
Address: 1010 Massachusetts Ave NW
Washington, DC 20001
Phone: (202) 320-9200

#366
Choong Man Chicken
Cuisines: Seafood, Korean, Chicken Wings
Average price: Modest
Area: H Street Corridor/Atlas District
Address: 1125 H St NE
Washington, DC 20002
Phone: (202) 399-6010

#367
Busboys And Poets - Takoma
Cuisines: American, Mediterranean,
Breakfast & Brunch
Average price: Modest
Area: Takoma
Address: 235 Carroll St NW
Washington, DC 20012
Phone: (202) 726-0856

#368
Morrison-Clark Restaurant
Cuisines: American
Average price: Modest
Area: Downtown
Address: 1011 L St NW
Washington, DC 20001
Phone: (202) 898-1200

#369
District Taco
Cuisines: Mexican
Average price: Inexpensive
Area: Capitol Hill
Address: 656 Pennsylvania Ave SE
Washington, DC 20003
Phone: (202) 735-5649

#370
Beuchert's Saloon
Cuisines: Bars, American,
Breakfast & Brunch
Average price: Modest
Area: Capitol Hill
Address: 623 Pennsylvania Ave SE
Washington, DC 20003
Phone: (202) 733-1384

#371
CAVA
Cuisines: Mediterranean
Average price: Modest
Area: Tenleytown
Address: 4237 Wisconsin Ave NW
Washington, DC 20016
Phone: (202) 695-8115

#372
Spicy Delight
Cuisines: Caribbean
Average price: Modest
Area: Takoma
Address: 308 Carroll St NW
Washington, DC 20012
Phone: (202) 829-9783

#373
Jam Doung Style Cuisine
Cuisines: Caribbean
Average price: Inexpensive
Area: Bloomingdale
Address: 1726 N Capitol St NW
Washington, DC 20002
Phone: (202) 483-2445

#374
Crepeaway
Cuisines: Creperies
Average price: Inexpensive
Area: Downtown
Address: 2001 L St NW
Washington, DC 20036
Phone: (202) 973-0404

#375
Noodles On 11
Cuisines: Noodles
Average price: Modest
Area: Downtown
Address: 1100 New York Ave NW
Washington, DC 20005
Phone: (202) 408-3377

#376
Blues Alley
Cuisines: Jazz & Blues, Cajun/Creole
Average price: Modest
Area: Georgetown
Address: 1073 Wisconsin Ave NW
Washington, DC 20007
Phone: (202) 337-4141

#377
Habesha Market And Carry-Out
Cuisines: Ethiopian, American
Average price: Modest
Area: Shaw
Address: 1919 9th St NW
Washington, DC 20001
Phone: (202) 232-1919

#378
Dirty Habit
Cuisines: Cocktail Bars,
Diners, Breakfast & Brunch
Average price: Expensive
Area: Penn Quarter
Address: 700 F St NW
Washington, DC 20004
Phone: (202) 783-6060

#379
Toro Toro
Cuisines: Latin American
Average price: Expensive
Area: Downtown
Address: 1300 I Eye St NW
Washington, DC 20005
Phone: (202) 682-9500

#380
St. Arnold's Mussel Bar
Cuisines: Bars, Seafood
Average price: Modest
Area: Cleveland Park
Address: 3433 Connecticut Ave NW
Washington, DC 20008
Phone: (202) 621-6719

#381
Boulangerie Christophe
Cuisines: Bakeries, French, Cafes
Average price: Modest
Area: Georgetown
Address: 1422 Wisconsin Ave NW
Washington, DC 20007
Phone: (202) 450-6344

#382
Breadsoda
Cuisines: Bars, Delis, Sandwiches
Average price: Modest
Area: Glover Park
Address: 2233 Wisconsin Ave NW
Washington, DC 20007
Phone: (202) 333-7445

#383
Carolina Kitchen
Cuisines: Southern
Average price: Modest
Area: Brentwood
Address: 2350 Washington Pl NE
Washington, DC 20018
Phone: (202) 733-1216

#384
Ben's Upstairs
Cuisines: Bars, Tapas, American
Average price: Modest
Area: H Street Corridor/Atlas District
Address: 1001 H St NE
Washington, DC 20002
Phone: (202) 733-2405

#385
Thai Tanic Restaurant
Cuisines: Thai
Average price: Modest
Area: Logan Circle, Downtown
Address: 1326 14th St NW
Washington, DC 20005
Phone: (202) 588-1795

#386
Sette Osteria
Cuisines: Italian
Average price: Modest
Area: Logan Circle
Address: 1634 14th St NW
Washington, DC 20009
Phone: (202) 290-1178

#387
Laredo
Cuisines: Mexican, Latin American
Average price: Modest
Area: Cleveland Park
Address: 3500 Connecticut Ave NW
Washington, DC 20008
Phone: (202) 966-2530

#388
Montmartre
Cuisines: French, Juice Bars,
Breakfast & Brunch
Average price: Modest
Area: Capitol Hill
Address: 327 7th St SE
Washington, DC 20003
Phone: (202) 544-1244

#389
Stoney's
Cuisines: Bars, American
Average price: Modest
Area: Logan Circle, Downtown
Address: 1433 P St NW
Washington, DC 20005
Phone: (202) 234-1818

#390
Bresca
Cuisines: American
Average price: Expensive
Area: U Street Corridor
Address: 1906 14th St NW
Washington, DC 20009
Phone: (202) 518-7926

#391
Bar-Cöde
Cuisines: American, Pizza
Average price: Modest
Area: Downtown
Address: 1101 17th St NW
Washington, DC 20036
Phone: (202) 955-9001

#392
Simple Bar & Grill
Cuisines: American, Sports Bars, Pizza
Average price: Modest
Area: Brightwood
Address: 5828 Georgia Ave NW
Washington, DC 20011
Phone: (202) 316-9171

#393
The Pinch
Cuisines: Dive Bars, Music Venues,
American
Average price: Modest
Area: Columbia Heights
Address: 3548 14th St NW
Washington, DC 20010
Phone: (202) 722-4440

#394
Moby Dick House Of Kabob
Cuisines: Middle Eastern,
Persian/Iranian, Mediterranean
Average price: Inexpensive
Area: Georgetown
Address: 1070 31st St NW
Washington, DC 20007
Phone: (202) 333-4400

#395
District Anchor
Cuisines: Bars, Seafood
Average price: Modest
Area: Downtown
Address: 1900 M St NW
Washington, DC 20036
Phone: (202) 466-7378

#396
Sichuan Express
Cuisines: Chinese
Average price: Inexpensive
Area: Downtown
Address: 1825 I St NW
Washington, DC 20006
Phone: (202) 466-2038

#397
Nuvegan Café
Cuisines: Vegan, Soul Food,
Breakfast & Brunch
Average price: Modest
Area: Park View
Address: 2928 Georgia Ave NW
Washington, DC 20001
Phone: (202) 232-1700

#398
Cornerstone Cafe
Cuisines: Buffets
Average price: Inexpensive
Area: Downtown
Address: 1501 M St NW
Washington, DC 20005
Phone: (202) 463-3911

#399
El Camino
Cuisines: Mexican
Average price: Modest
Area: Bloomingdale
Address: 108 Rhode Island Ave NW
Washington, DC 20001
Phone: (202) 847-0419

#400
NOOK
Cuisines: Food Court
Average price: Inexpensive
Area: Federal Triangle
Address: 1300 Pennsylvania Ave NW
Washington, DC 20229
Phone: (202) 898-1828

#401
Meridian Pint
Cuisines: Bars, American
Average price: Modest
Area: Columbia Heights
Address: 3400 11th St NW
Washington, DC 20010
Phone: (202) 588-1075

#402
Plume
Cuisines: American, Desserts
Average price: Exclusive
Area: Downtown, Dupont Circle
Address: 1200 16th St NW
Washington, DC 20036
Phone: (202) 448-2300

#403
Rice
Cuisines: Thai
Average price: Modest
Area: Logan Circle
Address: 1608 14th St NW
Washington, DC 20009
Phone: (202) 234-2400

#404
Smoked & Stacked
Cuisines: American, Sandwiches
Average price: Modest
Area: Shaw, Downtown
Address: 1239 9th St NW
Washington, DC 20001
Phone: (202) 465-4822

#405
The Tavern At The Henley Park
Cuisines: American
Average price: Modest
Area: Downtown
Address: 926 Massachusetts Ave NW
Washington, DC 20001
Phone: (202) 414-0500

#406
Byblos Deli
Cuisines: Middle Eastern
Average price: Inexpensive
Area: Cleveland Park
Address: 3414 Connecticut Ave NW
Washington, DC 20008
Phone: (202) 364-6549

#407
CAVA
Cuisines: Mediterranean
Average price: Inexpensive
Area: Noma
Address: 50 Massachusetts Avenue NE
Washington, DC 20002
Phone: (202) 536-2540

#408
Top Of The Yard Rooftop Bar
Cuisines: Sports Bars,
Burgers, Chicken Wings
Average price: Modest
Area: Navy Yard
Address: 1265 First St SE
Washington, DC 20003
Phone: (202) 800-1000

#409
Turning Natural
Cuisines: Vegetarian,
Juice Bars & Smoothies
Average price: Inexpensive
Area: Anacostia
Address: 2025 Martin Luther King Jr Ave SE
Washington, DC 20020
Phone: (202) 800-8828

#410
Catrachitos Deli
Cuisines: Mexican, Latin American
Average price: Inexpensive
Area: Park View
Address: 3555 Georgia Ave NW
Washington, DC 20010
Phone: (202) 200-0433

#411
Yang Market
Cuisines: Grocery, Delis
Average price: Inexpensive
Area: Eckington
Address: 138 U St NE
Washington, DC 20002
Phone: (202) 795-9778

#412
El Chucho
Cuisines: Mexican
Average price: Modest
Area: Columbia Heights
Address: 3313 11th St NW
Washington, DC 20010
Phone: (202) 290-3313

#413
Saint's Paradise Cafeteria
Cuisines: Soul Food, Cafeteria
Average price: Modest
Area: Shaw
Address: 601 M St NW
Washington, DC 20001
Phone: (202) 789-2289

#414
Vegaritos Vegan Restaurant
Cuisines: Mexican
Average price: Inexpensive
Area: Takoma
Address: 6904 4th St NW
Washington, DC 20012
Phone: (202) 882-8988

#415
Comet Ping Pong
Cuisines: Pizza
Average price: Modest
Area: Chevy Chase
Address: 5037 Connecticut Ave NW
Washington, DC 20008
Phone: (202) 364-0404

#416
Barley Mac
Cuisines: Bars, American
Average price: Modest
Area: Rosslyn
Address: 1600 Wilson Blvd
Arlington, VA 22209
Phone: (703) 372-9494

#417
Tonton Chicken
Cuisines: Chicken Wings
Average price: Inexpensive
Area: Downtown
Address: 1018 Vermont Ave NW
Washington, DC 20005
Phone: (202) 347-9072

#418
Yafa Grille
Cuisines: Middle Eastern,
Mediterranean, Halal
Average price: Inexpensive
Area: Downtown
Address: 1205 19th St NW
Washington, DC 20036
Phone: (202) 750-6689

#419
Rebellion
Cuisines: Bars, American
Average price: Modest
Area: Dupont Circle
Address: 1836 18th St Nw
Washington, DC 20009
Phone: (202) 299-0399

#420
Zentan Restaurant
Cuisines: Sushi Bars,
Japanese, Cocktail Bars
Average price: Expensive
Area: Downtown
Address: 1155 14th St NW
Washington, DC 20005
Phone: (202) 379-4366

#421
Shake Shack
Cuisines: Hot Dogs, Burgers,
Ice Cream & Frozen Yogurt
Average price: Modest
Area: Penn Quarter
Address: 800 F St NW
Washington, DC 20004
Phone: (202) 800-9930

#422
We, The Pizza
Cuisines: Pizza
Average price: Inexpensive
Area: Capitol Hill
Address: 305 Pennsylvania Ave SE
Washington, DC 20003
Phone: (202) 544-4008

#423
Pho 14
Cuisines: Vietnamese
Average price: Modest
Area: Columbia Heights
Address: 1436 Park Rd NW
Washington, DC 20010
Phone: (202) 986-2326

#424
Surfside
Cuisines: Tex-Mex, Caribbean
Average price: Modest
Area: Glover Park
Address: 2444 Wisconsin Ave NW
Washington, DC 20007
Phone: (202) 337-0004

#425
Justin's Cafe
Cuisines: American, Sports Bars, Pizza
Average price: Modest
Area: Navy Yard
Address: 1025 1st St SE
Washington, DC 20003
Phone: (202) 652-1009

#426
Red Toque Cafe
Cuisines: Indian, Pakistani
Average price: Inexpensive
Area: Shaw
Address: 1701 6th St NW
Washington, DC 20001
Phone: (202) 588-5516

#427
Ophelia's Fish House
Cuisines: Seafood
Average price: Modest
Area: Capitol Hill
Address: 501 8th St SE
Washington, DC 20003
Phone: (202) 543-1445

#428
Giovanni's Trattu
Cuisines: Italian, Venues, Seafood
Average price: Modest
Area: Dupont Circle, Downtown
Address: 1823 Jefferson Pl NW
Washington, DC 20036
Phone: (202) 452-4960

#429
Lupo Verde
Cuisines: Italian, Bars, Pizza
Average price: Expensive
Area: U Street Corridor
Address: 1401 T St NW
Washington, DC 20009
Phone: (202) 827-4752

#430
Sunrise Cafe
Cuisines: Greek, American
Average price: Inexpensive
Area: Downtown
Address: 1102 17th St NW
Washington, DC 20036
Phone: (202) 463-0032

#431
Laoban Dumplings
Cuisines: Dim Sum
Average price: Inexpensive
Area: Foggy Bottom
Address: 2000 Pennsylvania Ave NW
Washington, DC 20006
Phone: (202) 780-8746

#432
Station Kitchen & Cocktails
Cuisines: American,
Coffee & Tea, Cocktail Bars
Average price: Modest
Area: Dupont Circle
Address: 2015 Massachusetts Ave NW
Washington, DC 20036
Phone: (202) 770-3426

#433
The Prime Rib
Cuisines: Steakhouses
Average price: Exclusive
Area: Downtown
Address: 2020 K St NW
Washington, DC 20006
Phone: (202) 466-8811

#434
The Bottom Line
Cuisines: American, Dive Bars
Average price: Inexpensive
Area: Downtown
Address: 1716 I St NW
Washington, DC 20006
Phone: (202) 298-8488

#435
Jaleo
Cuisines: Spanish, Tapas Bars
Average price: Expensive
Area: Penn Quarter
Address: 480 7th St NW
Washington, DC 20004
Phone: (202) 628-7949

#436
El Rinconcito II
Cuisines: Latin American, Mexican
Average price: Modest
Area: Columbia Heights
Address: 1326 Park Rd
Washington, DC 20010
Phone: (202) 299-1076

#437
The Grist Mill
Cuisines: Southern, American
Average price: Modest
Area: Downtown
Address: 815 14th St NW
Washington, DC 20005
Phone: (202) 783-7800

#438
Pineapple & Pearls
Cuisines: Cafes, Coffee & Tea, American
Average price: Exclusive
Area: Capitol Hill
Address: 715 8th St SE
Washington, DC 20003
Phone: (202) 595-7375

#439
Calico
Cuisines: American, Cocktail Bars
Average price: Modest
Area: Shaw, Downtown
Address: 50 Blagden Aly NW
Washington, DC 20001
Phone: (202) 791-0134

#440
&Pizza
Cuisines: Pizza
Average price: Inexpensive
Area: U Street Corridor
Address: 1250 U St NW
Washington, DC 20009
Phone: (202) 733-1286

#441
Taqueria Los Compadres
Cuisines: Mexican
Average price: Inexpensive
Area: Mount Pleasant
Address: 3213 Mount Pleasant St NW
Washington, DC 20010
Phone: (202) 248-3227

#442
El Centro
Cuisines: Bars, Mexican
Average price: Modest
Area: Georgetown
Address: 1218 Wisconsin Ave NW
Washington, DC 20007
Phone: (202) 303-2100

#443
Bistro Bohem
Cuisines: Breakfast & Brunch, Modern
European, Diners
Average price: Modest
Area: Shaw
Address: 600 Florida Ave NW
Washington, DC 20001
Phone: (202) 735-5895

#444
Ari's Diner
Cuisines: Diners, Breakfast & Brunch
Average price: Modest
Area: Ivy City
Address: 2003 Fenwick St
Washington, DC 20002
Phone: (202) 290-1827

#445
Mission
Cuisines: Mexican, Cocktail Bars
Average price: Modest
Area: Dupont Circle
Address: 1606 20th St
Washington, DC 20009
Phone: (202) 525-2010

#446
Menomale Pizza Napoletana
Cuisines: Bars, Pizza
Average price: Modest
Area: Brookland
Address: 2711 12th St NE
Washington, DC 20018
Phone: (202) 248-3946

#447
The Coupe
Cuisines: Diners, Breakfast & Brunch
Average price: Modest
Area: Columbia Heights
Address: 3415 11th St NW
Washington, DC 20010
Phone: (202) 290-3342

#448
Vapiano M Street
Cuisines: Italian, Pizza, Bars
Average price: Modest
Area: Downtown
Address: 1800 M St NW
Washington, DC 20036
Phone: (202) 640-1868

#449
7th Hill Pizza Palisades
Cuisines: American, Pizza, Sandwiches
Average price: Modest
Area: Palisades
Address: 4885 Macarthur Blvd NW
Washington, DC 20007
Phone: (202) 506-2821

#450
Beefsteak
Cuisines: Vegetarian
Average price: Modest
Area: Tenleytown
Address: 4531 Wisconsin Ave NW
Washington, DC 20016
Phone: (202) 244-2529

#451
Cafe Berlin
Cuisines: German
Average price: Modest
Area: Capitol Hill
Address: 322 Massachusetts Ave NE
Washington, DC 20002
Phone: (202) 543-7656

#452
Rakuya
Cuisines: Asian Fusion,
Sushi Bars, Japanese
Average price: Modest
Area: Dupont Circle
Address: 1900 Q St NW
Washington, DC 20009
Phone: (202) 265-7258

#453
Millie's Spring Valley
Cuisines: Tacos, Beer Bar,
Breakfast & Brunch
Average price: Expensive
Area: Spring Valley
Address: 4866 Massachusetts Ave NW
Washington, DC 20016
Phone: (202) 733-5789

#454
Homeslyce
Cuisines: Pizza, Bars
Average price: Modest
Area: Downtown
Address: 2121 K St NW
Washington, DC 20037
Phone: (202) 559-1555

#455
Penny Whisky Bar
Cuisines: Whiskey Bars,
American, Cocktail Bars
Average price: Modest
Area: Chinatown
Address: 618 H St NW
Washington, DC 20001
Phone: (240) 381-0009

#456
Sushi Express
Cuisines: Japanese, Sushi Bars
Average price: Inexpensive
Area: Downtown
Address: 1990 K St NW
Washington, DC 20006
Phone: (202) 659-1955

#457
Southern Hospitality
Cuisines: Southern, American, Sandwiches
Average price: Modest
Area: Adams Morgan
Address: 1815 Adams Mill Rd NW
Washington, DC 20009
Phone: (202) 588-0411

#458
Bodega
Cuisines: Tapas Bars, Spanish
Average price: Modest
Area: Georgetown
Address: 3116 M St NW
Washington, DC 20007
Phone: (202) 333-4733

#459
Hunan Dynasty
Cuisines: Chinese
Average price: Modest
Area: Capitol Hill
Address: 215 Pennsylvania Ave SE
Washington, DC 20003
Phone: (202) 546-6161

#460
Shaw's Tavern
Cuisines: Gastropubs
Average price: Modest
Area: Shaw
Address: 520 Florida Ave NW
Washington, DC 20001
Phone: (202) 518-4092

#461
Taberna Del Alabardero
Cuisines: Spanish, Tapas Bars, Diners
Average price: Expensive
Area: Downtown
Address: 1776 Eye St NW
Washington, DC 20006
Phone: (202) 429-2200

#462
Yosaku Japanese Restaurant
Cuisines: Japanese, Sushi Bars
Average price: Modest
Area: Tenleytown
Address: 4712 Wisconsin Ave NW
Washington, DC 20016
Phone: (202) 363-4453

#463
Colada Shop
Cuisines: Coffee & Tea, Cuban, Cocktail Bars
Average price: Modest
Area: U Street Corridor
Address: 1405 T St NW
Washington, DC 20009
Phone: (202) 332-8800

#464
Kofuku
Cuisines: Ramen, Sushi Bars
Average price: Modest
Area: Chinatown
Address: 815 7th St NW
Washington, DC 20001
Phone: (202) 842-5088

#465
CAVA
Cuisines: Mediterranean
Average price: Inexpensive
Area: Navy Yard
Address: 52 M Street SE
Washington, DC 20003
Phone: (202) 536-2522

#466
Mezeh Mediterranean Grill
Cuisines: Mediterranean
Average price: Inexpensive
Area: Crystal City
Address: 2450 Crystal Dr
Arlington, VA 22202
Phone: (703) 685-9907

#467
Pop's Seabar
Cuisines: American, Dive Bars, Seafood
Average price: Modest
Area: Adams Morgan
Address: 1817 Columbia Rd NW
Washington, DC 20009
Phone: (202) 534-3933

#468
Tortilla Cafe
Cuisines: Mexican, Salvadoran,
Breakfast & Brunch
Average price: Inexpensive
Area: Capitol Hill
Address: 210 7th St SE
Washington, DC 20003
Phone: (202) 547-5700

#469
Beau Thai
Cuisines: Thai, Bars, Breakfast & Brunch
Average price: Modest
Area: Shaw
Address: 1550 7th St NW
Washington, DC 20001
Phone: (202) 536-5636

#470
The Atrium Restaurant
Cuisines: American, Steakhouses
Average price: Expensive
Area: West End, Downtown
Address: 1221 22nd St NW
Washington, DC 20037
Phone: (202) 872-1500

#471
Maggiano's Little Italy
Cuisines: Italian, Bars
Average price: Modest
Area: Friendship Heights
Address: 5333 Wisconsin Ave NW
Washington, DC 20015
Phone: (202) 966-5500

#472
Sushi Keiko
Cuisines: Japanese, Sushi Bars
Average price: Modest
Area: Glover Park
Address: 2309 Wisconsin Ave NW
Washington, DC 20007
Phone: (202) 333-3965

#473
Tanad Thai Cuisine
Cuisines: Thai, Vegan, Vegetarian
Average price: Modest
Area: Tenleytown
Address: 4912 Wisconsin Ave NW
Washington, DC 20016
Phone: (202) 966-0616

#474
Sprig And Sprout
Cuisines: Vietnamese,
Sandwiches, Gluten-Free
Average price: Modest
Area: Glover Park
Address: 2317 Wisconsin Ave NW
Washington, DC 20007
Phone: (202) 333-2569

#475
Uniontown Bar And Grill
Cuisines: American, Lounges, Cajun/Creole
Average price: Modest
Area: Anacostia
Address: 2200 Martin Luther King Jr Ave SE
Washington, DC 20020
Phone: (202) 450-2536

#476
Betsy
Cuisines: Belgian
Average price: Modest
Area: Capitol Hill
Address: 514 8th St SE
Washington, DC 20003
Phone: (202) 544-0100

#477
Smith Commons
Cuisines: Bars, American
Average price: Modest
Area: H Street Corridor/Atlas District
Address: 1245 H St NE
Washington, DC 20002
Phone: (202) 396-0038

#478
Johnny's Half Shell
Cuisines: Seafood
Average price: Modest
Area: Adams Morgan
Address: 1819 Columbia Rd NW
Washington, DC 20009
Phone: (202) 506-5257

#479
Commissary
Cuisines: American,
Breakfast & Brunch, Sandwiches
Average price: Modest
Area: Logan Circle, Downtown
Address: 1443 P St NW
Washington, DC 20005
Phone: (202) 299-0018

#480
&Pizza
Cuisines: Pizza
Average price: Inexpensive
Area: Chinatown
Address: 705 H St NW
Washington, DC 20001
Phone: (202) 558-7569

#481
Logan Tavern
Cuisines: Bars, American,
Breakfast & Brunch
Average price: Modest
Area: Logan Circle, Downtown
Address: 1423 P St NW
Washington, DC 20005
Phone: (202) 332-3710

#482
Micho's Lebanese Grill
Cuisines: Lebanese
Average price: Inexpensive
Area: H Street Corridor/Atlas District
Address: 500 H St NE
Washington, DC 20002
Phone: (202) 450-4533

#483
Chinatown Express
Cuisines: Chinese
Average price: Inexpensive
Area: Chinatown
Address: 746 6th St NW
Washington, DC 20001
Phone: (202) 638-0424

#484
Great Wall Szechuan House
Cuisines: Chinese
Average price: Modest
Area: Logan Circle
Address: 1527 14th St NW
Washington, DC 20005
Phone: (202) 797-8888

#485
China Town Carryout
Cuisines: Chinese
Average price: Inexpensive
Area: Mount Pleasant
Address: 3207 Mt Pleasant St NW
Washington, DC 20010
Phone: (202) 332-8955

#486
Cornercopia
Cuisines: Delis, Beer, Wine & Spirits
Average price: Inexpensive
Area: Navy Yard
Address: 1000 3rd St SE
Washington, DC 20003
Phone: (202) 525-1653

#487
Siren By RW
Cuisines: Seafood
Average price: Expensive
Area: Downtown, Logan Circle
Address: 1515 Rhode Island Ave NW
Washington, DC 20005
Phone: (202) 521-7171

#488
Naf Naf Grill
Cuisines: Falafel, Middle Eastern, Salad
Average price: Modest
Area: Downtown
Address: 1875 K St NW
Washington, DC 20006
Phone: (202) 618-3724

#489
Elizabeth's Gone Raw
Cuisines: Vegan, Live/Raw Food
Average price: Exclusive
Area: Downtown
Address: 1341 L St NW
Washington, DC 20005
Phone: (202) 347-8349

#490
**Chercher Ethiopian
Restaurant & Mart**
Cuisines: Ethiopian
Average price: Modest
Area: Shaw, Downtown
Address: 1334 9th St NW
Washington, DC 20001
Phone: (202) 798-6762

#491
Subbs By Carl
Cuisines: Sandwiches
Average price: Inexpensive
Area: Brookland
Address: 2208 Rhode Island Ave NE
Washington, DC 20018
Phone: (202) 529-6225

#492
Cusbah
Cuisines: Pakistani, Indian, American
Average price: Modest
Area: H Street Corridor/Atlas District
Address: 1128 H St NE
Washington, DC 20002
Phone: (202) 506-1504

#493
M Bar
Cuisines: Bars, Comfort Food
Average price: Modest
Area: Downtown
Address: 1143 New Hampshire Ave NW
Washington, DC 20037
Phone: (202) 775-0800

#494
New Big Wong Chinese Restaurant
Cuisines: Cantonese, Szechuan
Average price: Modest
Area: Chinatown
Address: 610 H St NW
Washington, DC 20001
Phone: (202) 628-0491

#495
**1230 Restaurant
& Champagne Lounge**
Cuisines: American, Lounges, French
Average price: Modest
Area: Shaw, Downtown
Address: 1230 9th St NW
Washington, DC 20001
Phone: (202) 567-1358

#496
Bourbon
Cuisines: Bars, American
Average price: Modest
Area: Adams Morgan
Address: 2321 18th St NW
Washington, DC 20009
Phone: (202) 332-0800

#497
Chalin's Restaurant
Cuisines: Chinese, Seafood, Soup
Average price: Modest
Area: Downtown
Address: 1912 I St NW
Washington, DC 20006
Phone: (202) 293-6000

#498
Froggy Bottom Pub
Cuisines: Vietnamese, American, Pubs
Average price: Modest
Area: Downtown
Address: 2021 K St NW
Washington, DC 20006
Phone: (202) 338-3000

#499
GW Delicatessen
Cuisines: Delis, Sandwiches, Bagels
Average price: Inexpensive
Area: Foggy Bottom
Address: 2133 G St NW
Washington, DC 20037
Phone: (202) 331-9391

#500
Kanji Kana Restaurant
Cuisines: Japanese, Salad, Soup
Average price: Modest
Area: Downtown
Address: 1018 Vermont Ave NW
Washington, DC 20005
Phone: (202) 393-4545

Printed in Great Britain
by Amazon